Tidewaters of the Connecticut River

*An Explorer's Guide
To Hidden Coves
and Marshes*

Written by
Thomas Maloney

and

Juliana Panos Barrett

Nels Barrett

Stephen Gephard

Geoffrey A. Hammerson

Carol Hardin Kimball

John Pfeiffer

Noble Proctor

Janet Radway Stone

First Edition
Printed and bound in East Windsor, Connecticut
by Impressions, Inc.

Art by *David Dunlop*

Cover and Book Design by *Rhode van Gessel Weiner*

Edited by *River's End Press*

Maps by *River's End Press*

Published by *River's End Press, L.L.C.*
Jennifer R. McCann, managing member
Old Saybrook, Connecticut

Resource List by
Amy Cabaniss

All profits from the sale of this book go
to the Connecticut River Watershed Council
for the conservation and protection
of the Connecticut River.

Art and Photo Credits and Permissions
Nels Barrett: 16; 44; Robert Benson: 11; 12; 13; 14; 15; 24; 51; 57; 63; 68;
92; 93; Diane Blasius: 25; Connecticut River Museum: 7; 8; 62; Deep River
Historical Society: 75; David Dunlop: Front and Back Cover; 5; 37; 43; 49;
55; 61; 67; 73; 79; 85; 91; 97; 103; Frank Gallo: 17; 18; 19; Hank Golet: 26;
Blair Nikula: 29; Old Saybrook Historical Society: 99; Robert Perron: 1; 3;
28; Judy Preston: 38; 56; 74; 86; 104; Abigail Rorer: 59; 71; 83; 95; 101; 107;
Joel Stocker: 87; Janet Stone: 2; The Nature Conservancy: 16; 19; 21; 22; 27;
Valley Railroad: 81

This book is dedicated to

Roger Tory Peterson
and Edmund Delaney

*for their singular contributions
to our understanding and appreciation
of the natural and cultural heritage
of the Tidewaters region*

Contents

Contents

Foreword

THIS THOROUGHLY RESEARCHED and informative guide to the tidewaters of the Connecticut River brings back a host of memories to an old sailor and river explorer like myself.

Forty years ago and more we acquired a 20 foot catboat, which we named *Lady Fenwick* after that lovely, auburn-haired Englishwoman who came to the Saybrook Colony in 1639 with her husband George Fenwick, the second governor of the river Connecticut. A centerboarder, she tested the bottom of the river in many places, especially its creeks and marshlands. Summer and fall, she was our means of poking about— gunkholing, sailors call it. We tied our anchor line to a hemlock in Selden Creek; explored the Salmon River, "a sweet stream," as the poet John Brainard wrote, where "the Indian Magi made their spells by moonlight"; sailed upriver to attend a performance at the Goodspeed Opera House; cruised through the tall grasses of the Lyme marshes watching for herons, ospreys, and muskrats; even journeyed all the way to Hartford as if we were Adriaen Block, the Dutchman who discovered the "Long Tidal River" in 1614.

At that time I was oblivious to the great river's abuse and decline. The "ecology" movement had not even been born. In Connecticut it began in 1962 with the seminal report of William H. Whyte, who proposed a comprehensive plan for preserving and developing the state's natural resources. The Connecticut River, he pointed out, "is the most underexploited resource potential in the East...If pollution enforcement is really stepped up, the benefits will be incalculable."

My interest in pollution was really aroused after attending a conference in Hartford the next year, at which the Commissioner of Health declared that for more than 60 years the river had not been fit for fishing, swimming, or recreation because of the high coliform bacteria count. Its official classification was "suitable for transportation of sewage and industrial wastes." This once fair stream had become "a beautifully landscaped cesspool." That inspired me to get out my old Cine-Kodak camera and begin making a documentary on the river's history, beauty, and desecration.

Its soiled reputation had spread far and wide. I remember a story that Katharine Hepburn, who narrated the film, told when she made "Summertime" in Venice. One scene called for her to fall backward into the Grand Canal. David Lean, the director, said: "Kate, the water is so foul, I'm going to use your understudy." She shot back: "Not at all, you forget I was raised at the mouth of the Connecticut River!"

The widely shown film was a catalyst for action. In October 1965 Governor John Dempsey appointed a 100-man task force, which submitted a report with 32 recommendations the following May. Without a dissenting vote, the General Assembly passed the Clean Water Act on May 1, 1967. It authorized $150 million in bonds for building secondary treatment plants along the state's major rivers. By 1980, only 13 years later, nearly half of the stream miles on the Connecticut River and its tributaries within the state had been restored to Class B—that is, swimmable—and shad, striped bass, even a few Atlantic salmon, and other species were returning in greater numbers. Another environmental victory was won in 1969 with adoption of the Save the Wetlands Act.

Today's explorer of the river may not realize its past importance as a highway for trade and travel in the lower Connecticut Valley. For almost 200 years, in small towns from Old Saybrook to Windsor, dozens of family-owned shipyards handcrafted thousands of wooden sailing vessels that carried a variety of foodstuffs, livestock, and goods far and wide. These same villages also produced "men of iron" who became risk-taking merchants and courageous captains of privateers, packets, and merchantmen.

Little remains to be seen of the golden era of shipbuilding, except the stately homes of a few river captains. Yet, were they to return in their schooners and barks, they could still see and admire the salty marshes, the Great Meadow of Essex full of migratory birds, the hurricane refuge of Hamburg Cove, the eminence of Joshua's Rock, the hills known as the Seven Sisters in Hadlyme, the Middletown gorge, and the grassy floodplain stretching almost all the way to Windsor.

The absence of excessive development is due to several factors, not the least of which are the private ownership of riverfront properties for generations and, more recently, the conservation efforts of local land trusts, the Connecticut River Watershed Council, The Nature Conservancy, the Gateway Commission, and the Department of Environmental Protection. No wonder that the Connecticut River has been designated as one of 14 American Heritage Rivers and its tidal wetlands as one of 40 "Last Great Places" in the United States!

However, we cannot for a moment rest content with what has been achieved to reclaim and preserve our greatest natural resource. There are still challenges to be met and threats to be resisted. The downside of making the river a recreation highway is that it will become saturated with pleasure boats. Our marinas are already crowded. Yet people must have access to the river. The two best ways of accommodating them are cruise boats and riverfront parks, such as the ones being created in Old Saybrook, Deep River, East Hartford, and Hartford. In the Tidewaters the priorities are to protect the River's tributaries, especially the Black Hall, Eightmile, and Lieutenant rivers, and to restore the native plants by eliminating the invasive *Phragmites* reed.

Tidewaters of the Connecticut River is a valuable contribution to our understanding of the importance of a complete ecosystem for sustaining the life of those who live around it, not only in our generation but for generations to come.

– Ellsworth S. Grant

Introduction

EACH OF US HAS A SPECIAL PLACE, a place of such beauty and special quality that it inspires us as much in memory as it does in experience. For the authors of this guidebook, that special place is the tidal estuary of the Connecticut River—the Tidewaters region—and its many coves and inlets. Brought together by their common love and respect for these many-faceted environmental jewels, they created **Tidewaters of the Connecticut River: An Explorer's Guide to Hidden Coves and Marshes** to share their knowledge and appreciation with you and to give you the tools with which to discover and experience each of the coves for yourself. Their essays on geology, history, fish, birds, flora, and fauna provide insight into what you will see and why, and are preface to twelve guided tours for you to do on your own. As you read each of the chapters, think of yourself as part of a conversation among friends and colleagues whose personal and professional lives are dedicated to interpreting and conserving the rich and diverse resources—cultural and environmental—of this singular, special place.

A Watershed Context

The Tidewaters region of the Connecticut River is the end point of New England's largest river ecosystem. The river begins at Fourth Connecticut Lake, a small open-water wetland at the Canadian border, and flows south for 410 miles to Long Island Sound at Old Saybrook. Its watershed includes significant parts of four states—New Hampshire, Vermont, Massachusetts and Connecticut—a total of over 11,000 square miles.

Long appreciated locally as a source of food, transportation, and power, the Connecticut River has gained increasing national recognition for its extraordinary natural and cultural values. In 1991, President George Bush recognized the national significance of the unique environmental resources of the Connecticut River watershed by signing legislation to establish the Silvio O. Conte National Fish and Wildlife Refuge, the only national refuge encompassing an entire watershed ecosystem. Seven years later, President Bill Clinton designated the Connecticut as one of only 14 American Heritage Rivers, a singular honor that recognizes rivers with combined cultural, economic, and environmental significance.

Conserving Natural Values

The Tidewaters region is the crown jewel of the Connecticut River watershed, unmatched for its natural and cultural assets. It was recognized by the U.S. Fish & Wildlife Service in 1991 as one of the richest wetland ecosystems in the northeastern United States. In 1993, it was designated as one of the 40 "Last Great Places" in the hemisphere by The Nature Conservancy, one of the nation's leading nonprofit conservation organizations. And it was acclaimed in 1994 as containing "Wetlands of International Importance" under an international treaty to conserve unique, high-value wetlands, known as the "Ramsar Convention."

This modern recognition of conservation values hides three centuries of abuse. From the mid-17th to the mid-20th century, tidal wetlands were dredged, filled, dammed, ditched, and channelized, all in the name of "progress." The Connecticut River itself was so polluted from wastes dumped throughout its length that an editorial writer a half century ago called it "the best landscaped sewer in the nation."

Two things saved the Connecticut River and its tidal wetlands from total ruin—the river itself and positive human intervention. The physical nature of the river creates shifting sandbars as it empties into Long Island Sound, a natural impediment to all but shallow–draft boats and barges. With no opportunity for a deepwater port, the Connecticut is one of the few major rivers on the East Coast without a major city and surrounding urban sprawl at its mouth. As a result, there was little development pressure to justify the expense of filling all wetlands. The pollution that so degraded the river and threatened many of its dependent species has been significantly reduced by environmental laws passed since the 1960s by the U.S. Congress and enacted by the four watershed states in response to advocates for clean water. Communities and industries that once used the river as a place to dump wastes now help to protect it. Species in peril of extinction—ospreys, bald eagles, Atlantic salmon, and others—are being restored by individuals, citizen groups, and government, taking action to protect and enhance key habitats. The river also has a champion—the Connecticut River Watershed Council—a citizen group founded in 1952 at the height of the river's pollution problems to push for its cleanup and restoration.

Several of the conservation actions affecting the Tidewaters region warrant mention. (A complete account would take a book in its own right, and it is equally impossible to credit the countless individuals who have devoted their lives to protecting the river's natural and cultural assets.) The conservation ethic of the communities and residents of the Tidewaters region led to the creation of local land trusts that were the pioneers of the land trust movement of the last quarter century. These volunteer groups work with individual landowners to protect open space and critical natural areas; to date, they have protected nearly 3,000 acres. This ethic—and an increasing appreciation of the region's unique scenic, ecological, scientific, and historic values—led to local support for the creation of the Connecticut River Gateway Commission by the Connecticut General Assembly in 1973. The Commission was given a regional delegation of local authority that allows it to review and approve new development within sight of the river. Special recognition is due to the Connecticut Chapter of The Nature Conservancy for its Tidelands Program, which has helped to ensure the protection of Griswold Point, Chapman's Pond, Selden Creek, and Lord Cove, and is working to conserve additional lands.

The Connecticut Department of Environmental Protection and the U.S. Fish & Wildlife Service have been responsible for the restoration of threatened populations of birds and fish. Their actions have been matched by local groups and individuals who have erected the osprey nesting platforms seen throughout the Tidewaters region, and by the migratory fisheries restoration initiative of the Connecticut River Watershed Council, which works in partnership with federal, state, and community agencies and local groups to restore access to critical tributary spawning habitats.

On the cultural side of the ledger, there is the Connecticut River Museum and the many local historical societies that protect and interpret the rich heritage of this region. Finally, there are the staffs and members of the Connecticut River Estuary Regional Planning Agency and the town boards and commissions that oversee countless individual development decisions to ensure that the public's interest in clean water, open space, river access, and rural quality of life are protected. Thank you all.

The Future

Protecting the coves and wetlands of the Tidewaters region is a continuous effort. The very things that led to the writing of this guidebook—the beauty of the lower Connecticut River and the ecological richness of its coves— are attracting ever more people and more development. Without care and vigilance, too many people, too many boats, and just a few ill-sited houses could seriously damage, and perhaps even destroy, the Tidewaters' special qualities. A growing prevalence of non-native invasive plants and animals also threatens to harm the ecology of the coves. Fortunately, there are many people working to ensure that that does not happen. They include federal, state, and local governments, nonprofit citizen groups, landowners, and businesses. They should include everyone who uses and enjoys the Connecticut River and its tidal coves.

There are two important messages contained in this guidebook. The first is how to understand and enjoy the Tidewaters region of the Connecticut River. The second is an exhortation to become involved. You can help to protect these remarkable coves and wetlands. When you visit, do so with as little impact as possible. Become a member of the organizations working to protect these natural areas and increase our understanding of them. Volunteer to serve on a community board or advisory committee, and attend public hearings to let those local agencies know you support—and sometimes demand—their efforts to protect the environmental and cultural assets of your community. Learn how to be a good steward of your own land, and if you live in the Tidewaters region, understand that what you do has a direct effect on the Connecticut River and all its natural resources.

Welcome to the Tidewaters region of the Connecticut River.

Tom Miner
Executive Director
Connecticut River Watershed Council

Acknowledgments

THIS BOOK WAS SPARKED in the minds of many whose love and knowledge of the river came together at the same time. The initial idea was just a small part of the finished product; endless hours of volunteered time, donated writing, graphics, and artwork, speak volumes of the contributors' dedication to the river. Thanks foremost to them. Ultimately it is the river that will benefit from this dedication—as monies generated by the sales of this book will support work to conserve, restore and protect the Connecticut River. Sincere thanks go to David Dunlop, whose beautiful oil paintings grace these pages. His generosity in donating these paintings for sale as a fund-raiser enabled the color production of this book. His enthusiasm for the Connecticut River will multiply in the hearts of all who view his artwork.

Many thanks go out to the individuals who provided additional support through photographs and illustrations, including Nels Barrett, Robert Benson, Frank Gallo, Stephen Gephard, Hank Golet, Blair Nikula, Judy Preston, Robert Perron, Joel Stocker, Diane Blasius, Marc Nodden, and Ralph Hermann. A number of people also contributed to the editing of the book, refining it from a collection of papers to a finished product: John Surowiecki, Thomas Miner, Thomas Maloney, Stephen Gephard, Carol Hardin Kimball, Geoffrey A. Hammerson, Ashley Prout and Norma Roche. Also, the help and expertise of the following organizations were invaluable: the Connecticut River Watershed Council, The Nature Conservancy, the Connecticut River Estuary Regional Planning Agency, Connecticut Department of Environmental Protection, Marine Fisheries Division, The Connecticut River Museum, and the Valley Railroad.

In addition, warm thanks are due to numerous land trust and historical society members, librarians, and longtime residents of the various towns for their assistance in pointing the writer of the historical notes in the right direction, digging up useful information, telling stories of olden times, and loaning family papers and photographs. The following people generously made available their own original research: Carolyn Bakke Bacdayan (Sterling City), Stephen Gephard (Chapman Pond), Jim Leatherbee (Hadlyme/Whalebone Cove), Donald Malcarne (Essex), Charlot Pike (on behalf of Deep River Navigation), Elizabeth Huey Putnam (Brockway Landing), Joel P. Severance (Chester Creek), David H. Wordell (Selden Island), and Linda H. Winzer (Hadlyme).

Lastly, thanks to all friends, family, and associates who lent patience, a sympathetic ear, and encouragement from the beginning to the end of the process. It's proven well worth the effort!

Jennifer R. McCann
River's End Press

Tidewaters of the Connecticut River

Part I
A Regional Overview

Chapter 1
Geology

Janet Radway Stone

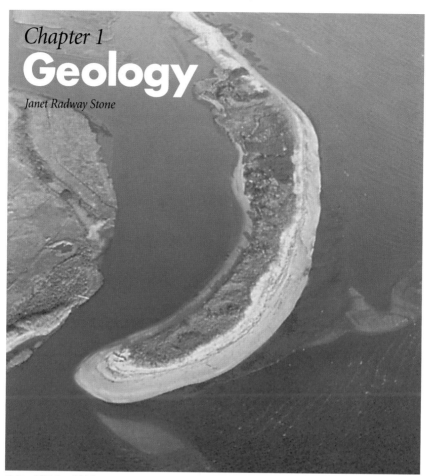

Griswold Point, Old Lyme

Courtesy of Robert Perron

he upper reaches of the Connecticut River form the boundary between New Hampshire and Vermont, lying in a valley flanked by the White and Green Mountains. The river then flows south through Massachusetts and northern Connecticut in the Connecticut Valley, a broad central lowland that geologists call the Hartford Rift Basin, which is underlain by easily eroded sedimentary rocks (shale and sandstone) locally known as "brownstone." Over its 410-mile journey from Fourth Connecticut Lake to Long Island Sound, the river drops over 2,600 feet in elevation.

There is a popular myth that the river once flowed to New Haven. While the Hartford Rift Basin does extend to the New Haven area, there is no geological evidence that the river went that way. In fact, erosion-resistant basalt (or "traprock") ridges extending from Hartford

south to Middletown prevent the river from following the southward course to New Haven.

Crashing into Avalonia

At Middletown, the Connecticut River turns eastward and flows southeast to Old Saybrook in a narrow, bedrock-walled valley cut through older metamorphic rocks. The hills that flank the river valley are the eroded remnants of rocks that were heated and metamorphosed about 300 million years ago when the ancient continents of North America, Africa, Eurasia, and the island continent of Avalonia all collided and formed the supercontinent called Pangea.

When the landmasses pulled apart, 100 million years later, a small section of Avalonia remained welded to Connecticut and Massachusetts while its bulk adhered to Africa. This continental

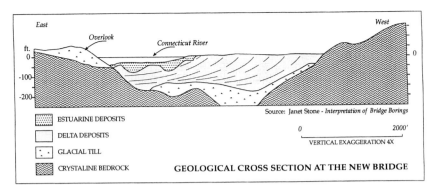

East		West

ESTUARINE DEPOSITS

DELTA DEPOSITS

GLACIAL TILL

CRYSTALINE BEDROCK

Source: Janet Stone - *Interpretation of Bridge Borings*

VERTICAL EXAGGERATION 4X

GEOLOGICAL CROSS SECTION AT THE NEW BRIDGE

"fender bender" made Avalonia a permanent resident of southeastern Connecticut. The line marking this junction, called the Honey Hill fault, runs under the Connecticut River between Deep River and Lyme. Rock ridges containing broad bands of gneiss, schist, and granite were brought to their present alignment during the continental collision; today, they provide a striking backdrop to the Tidewaters region.

The Ice Age

The modern-day Connecticut River has developed over the past 2 million years. During this time, continental ice sheets repeatedly advanced into New England from the north. The most recent reached its terminal position at Long Island 22,000 years ago; it began its northward retreat about 2,000 years later. The glacial ice covered all of New England and was at least a mile thick over central Connecticut. Its tremendous weight (more than 200 tons per square foot) depressed the earth's crust by hundreds of feet. The enormous quantity of water bound up in this much ice lowered worldwide sea levels by at least 400 feet.

The advance and retreat of the last ice sheet defined many details of the modern river valley. During glacial advance, ice scoured the bedrock surface, deepening the valley, and deposited glacial till locally on the hillsides. During retreat, debris-laden melt-water streams flowing from the ice front deposited sands and gravels in the river valley. Near the mouth of the Connecticut River in Old Saybrook and Old Lyme several low ridges, or moraines, formed from glacial debris deposited along

the ice front when the northward retreat of the glacier stalled. The north side of the peninsula at Fenwick on the west side of the river's mouth is an example of a recessional moraine. Other low-lying surfaces near the mouth of the river, such as Saybrook Point and the south part of Fenwick, are sand and gravel deltas built by melt-water streams as they flowed into a large glacial lake that occupied what is now Long Island Sound. The remains of these deltas form the foundation of the marsh system found here today.

Flat-topped terraces of glacial sand and gravel deposited as deltas flank the river along the entire length of the lower valley. These terraces increase in height from about 25 feet above water level at the mouth of the river to about 150 feet in Portland. You can see a preserved portion of one of these deltas about 35 feet above water level on the west side of the river just north of the Baldwin Bridge. Other examples can be found at Chester and Hadlyme, where they stand 55 feet above river level, and on the west side of the river at the East Haddam Bridge, at 85 feet above the river.

Meltdown and rebound

Many aspects of today's river course are due to the response of the land and sea to the melting of the glacier. As the last glacial ice sheet retreated northward, many glacial lakes were formed; some of them were quite large. Glacial Lake Connecticut occupied the present-day Long Island Sound and tidewater estuary. Farther north in the Connecticut Valley, delta sands and gravels built into glacial Lake

Middletown dammed the bedrock valley between Rocky Hill and Glastonbury, creating glacial Lake Hitchcock, which extended more than 150 miles up the Connecticut River valley.

Glacial Lake Connecticut in Long Island Sound slowly drained away and was gone by about 15,000 years ago. Due to the melting of the ice sheet, worldwide sea levels slowly rose and flooded the drained lake basin in Long Island Sound. By about 13,500 years ago, enough glacial ice had melted that the earth's crust, unburdened by the tremendous weight of the ice, began to rebound. This occurred rapidly enough to keep the land above the rising sea level in Long Island Sound. The initiation of rebound also caused the dam at Rocky Hill to break, allowing glacial Lake Hitchcock to drain. Once the glacial lakes had drained, the post-glacial Connecticut River established itself on the drained lakebed, cutting deeply into the lake sediments. Multiple terrace levels formed by downcutting of the river can be seen in the upper valley.

By 4,000 years ago, sea level had risen to about 25 feet below modern levels. Former floodplain surfaces along the coast and in the lower river valley were inundated and subjected to daily rise and fall of tides. Extensive tidal marshes developed on exposed surfaces, the mouth of the river became an estuary, and tidal effects reached far upstream. Tides and currents produced shifting sandbars where the river meets the sound, creating a future barrier to deep-draft ships.

Tidal marshes also formed at the mouths of tributary streams and rivers. These once carried great loads of glacial outwash, which today forms the foundation for some of the freshwater tidal marshes, such as Pratt and Post coves and Salmon Cove. These sites will continue to evolve as the marshes accumulate vegetation and organic muds and as sea level continues to rise.

River hydrology

The tidal regime and the annual flood cycles of the river determine much of the ecology of the Tidewaters region. As a result of its immense watershed–some 11,260 square miles–the Connecticut River delivers 70 percent of Long Island Sound's freshwater. Flows fluctuate from about 29 billion gallons per day during the spring freshet in April to average August low flows of about 4.5 billion gallons per day. This flooding regime has an effect on the habitats in the Tidewaters region through its influence on the plant communities. The volume of water also carries tremendous quantities of sediment, much of which settles out in the lower river valley. The sediment and varying flows create a river's mouth that is ever changing.

Aerial view of the Lieutenant River and Saybrook Point

Courtesy of Robert Perron

Tidal flows of saltwater from Long Island Sound also affect the Tidewaters region, determining what plants, fishes, and animals live where. High tides occur twice each day, about a half hour later each cycle. Their effect on the flow of the Connecticut River is seasonal. The volume of freshwater discharged during the spring freshet is so great that tidal fluctuations have almost no effect, and there is an absence of salinity in the surface waters at the mouth of the river. During lower flows, tidal fluctuation of river level is noticeable upstream as far north as Windsor Locks. The salt front—the point at which the river's surface waters change from fresh to brackish—is normally around Nott Island, but it can extend as far upstream as Eustasia Island in times of drought.

A geological history of continental collisions, ice ages, and mighty floods is responsible for the rich diversity of coves, plants, and animals that exists today. Our knowledge of that history only increases our respect for the natural forces that have shaped our world and created such wondrous places for us to explore as the hidden marshes and coves of the Tidewaters region.

To help boaters plan their trips to the Tidewaters region, Table I displays the average tidal flux at selected locations along the river.

TABLE I. High Tide Time Delay and Average Tidal Flux

FROM HIGH WATER AT SAYBROOK LIGHTHOUSE

High Tide at	Time *(high water from Saybrook)*	Mean *(feet)*	Spring *(feet)*
Saybrook Point	10 minutes	3.2	3.8
Old Lyme, *(Baldwin Bridge)*	24 minutes	3.1	3.7
Essex	38 minutes	3.0	3.6
Hadlyme	1 hour, 18 minutes	2.7	3.2
East Haddam	1 hour, 41 minutes	2.9	3.5
Haddam	1 hour, 47 minutes	2.5	3.0
Higganum Creek	1 hour, 54 minutes	2.6	3.1
Portland	2 hours, 50 minutes	2.2	2.6

Adapted from *"Investigating the Marine Environment: A Sourcebook,* Vol ll, by Howard Weiss and Michael Dorsey

Chapter 2
Prehistory and History

John Pfeiffer

North Cove, **Essex**

Art courtesy of David Dunlop

Approximately 10,000 years ago, several thousand years after the glacial retreat, early Paleo–Americans settled in the lower Connecticut River valley. At the time, the environment was comparable to that of the tundras far to our north in Labrador and on the Canadian Shield. Stone tools found in Lyme, Old Lyme, Hadlyme, Haddam, East Haddam, and Lebanon suggest that the early Native Americans were nomadic hunters and gatherers whose travels may have extended over several hundred miles in the course of one year. These nomadic Paleo-Americans followed migratory herds, such as woodland caribou, and adapted to the seasonal availability of other animal and plant species.

Some time later, the climate warmed and the population of herding animals decreased, replaced by more solitary animal species. In this new world, hunting and gathering replaced the nomadic lifestyle. Hunters had to readjust to a newly forested environment and less predictable nonherding animals. They then began counting on reliable, seasonal food sources such as migratory birds and fish. Communities were now situated along ponds, lakes, and streams. In fact, glacial kettle ponds appear to have been a favored location for these 6,000–10,000 year-old communities. Several have been found in the Old Lyme and Lyme area. The most significant known site of this period, however, is the Dill Farm site in East Haddam, overlooking Pine Brook and a prehistoric lake that existed between 6,000 and 12,000 years ago. The site appears to have been occupied for several thousand years and was vacated by prehistoric peoples only when the lake filled.

The Archaic period

The prehistory of the lower Connecticut from approximately 6,000 years ago is divided into Archaic and Woodland periods. It began with Native Americans developing their own cultures, identities, and territories, and it ended with the "first contact" with Europeans in the 15th century. In the Later Archaic period (3,700 to 6,000 years ago), hunting played an important role in the life of Native American communities. Even so, there is substantial evidence that these peoples gathered plant materials and collected shellfish. Their storage technology was advanced, which suggests that they were no longer solely dependent upon seasonal food and tended to stay in one place year-round.

At this time, the idea of territory came into play. Villages were identified as the home of distinct groups, and for the first time, burial grounds were located near the village sites as a way to show territorial rights over generations. At a 5,000-year-old site in Old Lyme, a village was uncovered  with wigwam outlines, storage pits, many artifacts, and a cremation burial ground.

In the Terminal Archaic period, approximately 2,700 to 3,700 years ago, part of the Native American population spread across the river's floodplain. In this floodplain culture, village life became less communal. Individual family residence units were more important as people came together strictly for ceremonial and social functions. Sites in Old Lyme, Old Saybrook, Lyme, Deep River, East Haddam, and Haddam have documented the Connecticut floodplain culture (the Griffin site in Old Lyme shows the remains of a very lavish burial ceremony). Life for the floodplain people, however, was quite stressful. Other groups outside the lowlands were hostile, and rising sea levels made the floodplain a much less attractive place to live.

By 2,700 years ago, groups from the neighboring uplands displaced the floodplain people. What became of them is not known. Whether they relocated, died off, or were killed by hostile groups remains a mystery.

The Woodland period

Those Native Americans who remained after the disappearance of the floodplain culture represent the Woodland period culture. The Early Woodland period (2,000 to 2,700 years ago) was marked by the invention of ceramics and a new weapon, the bow and arrow. Sites were small, and their residents appeared to be employed in a wide array of activities. The Middle Woodland period (1,000 to 2,000 years ago) showed a continuation of cultural patterns with refinements in ceramic technology and suggestions of communication—and even trade—with people outside the Connecticut River valley. The Late Woodland period (400 to 1,000 years ago) was marked by the addition of agriculture to the pre-existing gathering and hunting lifestyle. The maintenance of farm plots for the production of corn, beans, and squash meant that villages were occupied for extended periods of time and were abandoned only when the soil became exhausted or when sources of firewood were too distant. Late Woodland settlements and villages were common along the lower river. Late Woodland habitations dotted the coastline and riverbanks, and social interaction among neighboring villages and regions was commonplace. In other parts of the Northeast, Late Woodland villages were very large, unlike those in the lower Connecticut River valley. The reason is unclear. All we know for certain is that the cultural development of the lower river peoples was cut short by contact with Europeans, who brought with them diseases such as smallpox and influenza, against which the native peoples had not developed immunity. Epidemics resulted in a horrifying 95 percent population reduction.

First contact: The Dutch

The exact date of first contact with Europeans is not known. However, it's certain that a number of 16th-century traders, fishermen, and travelers passed by our shores and perhaps even investigated the lower river. Settlement by Europeans is another matter, and evidence suggests a Dutch presence in the Connecticut River valley immediately after Adriaen Block's 1614 voyage through Long Island Sound. Dutch trading stations were constructed at the mouth of the river (they called it the Fresh River) at Saybrook Point and another was maintained upriver in what is now Hartford. The Dutch accurately mapped the lower Connecticut River and its tributaries.

The English and Saybrook Colony

English settlement in the lower Connecticut River valley began in 1635 for both political and economic reasons. The Saybrook Colony, established at the mouth of the Connecticut, was intended primarily as a safe haven for Puritan refugees fleeing Charles I. A Puritan engineer, Lion Gardiner, was sent to the lower river region to dislodge the Dutch and to establish up to nine forts. One was built at the mouth of the river at Saybrook Point and was maintained into the 18th century. Whether any of the other intended forts were ever built is still vague, although there is some evidence that one may have existed in Lyme.

Economically, the establishment of Saybrook Colony was important in order to reinforce English control of the flow of timber from the Connecticut Valley. Wood used for building and heating was of critical importance to the early European settlers. Considered a luxury in Europe, wood was shipped to the mother country as well as to the West Indies. In fact, the very first issue addressed by the Connecticut Colonial Assembly was monitoring and restricting shipment of timber, plank, and staves, since the traffic in those goods aboard Dutch and English privateer vessels was eluding officials.

In 1637, the Pequots were, with bloody efficiency, eliminated as a threat to the English settlement. Four years later, Charles I was overthrown and the interim government of Oliver Cromwell was established. Those two events marked dramatic changes in the activities of the Puritan colony in the lower river area. Agriculture and the export of wood became increasingly important to the economic life of the region.

Throughout the lower valley, nearly every swift-running stream was dammed to power grist mills and sawmills. They not only ground corn and wheat, but they also cut and milled wood. In the middle of the 17th century, wood (and to a lesser degree, iron) continued to be an important mainstay of colonial exportation. Trade with England and the Caribbean islands continued for nearly 200 years, with agricultural products as exports and molasses and African slaves as imports.

The industrial plantation

By the early 18th century, businessmen had learned there was more profit in

Ely's Ferry

Courtesy of the Connecticut River Museum

Middle Cove: Schooner launching at the David Mack Shipyard   Courtesy of the Connecticut River Museum

manufacturing than in directly exporting raw material. Riverside sawmills were expanded to contain building yards, ironworks, and ship's stores where finished materials could be sold and exported. These businesses soon became self-sufficient colonial industrial plantations.

The lower Connecticut River valley soon became a home for shipbuilders, ship investors, and merchants. The wealth generated from these entrepreneurial activities established the lower valley as a major mercantile center in the American colonies. Local ships maintained close trading relations with Nova Scotia, Bermuda, and the West Indies, as well as England. Some were also involved in privateering.

The ventures of the privateers

Privateers would leave the ports of Lyme, Saybrook, Essex, and Deep River and venture out onto the high seas, where they would steal cargo from other vessels. The materials would be brought back to a local port, advertised in the newspapers, and sold at public auction. The colonial (and later American) authorities condoned this activity, since they received a certain percentage of the "take" for their support. Even in the 19th century privateering was big business. In fact, it was one of the causes of the War of 1812 with England. Finally, in 1814, the English delivered a severe blow to the privateer fleet in Essex, destroying 28 ships—the greatest financial loss ever inflicted by a foreign power on American soil until Pearl Harbor.

The new American industry

In 1815, a severe hurricane struck Essex with ferocious winds and a 20-foot storm surge that destroyed what the English had left behind the year before. Shipping in the lower river valley never completely recovered. New sources of material became available farther west and other modes of transportation became competitive. Still, while shipbuilding and shipping declined, the valley mill plantations did not lie idle. Mill sites became ever more specialized in manufacturing. American industry found a fertile place in which to grow in the Connecticut River valley. Thread, cloth and carpeting, shoes, furniture, iron and bronze fastenings, firearms, machinery, farming tools, silverware, and ivory objects (including combs and piano keys) were manufactured in the lower river valley region. Because of a shortage of labor, many of these operations initially employed freed slaves and remaining Native Americans as industrial workers. The valley became a major industrial center well known throughout the growing nation.

Parallel to the development of industry along the lower river, there was a steady transition from sailing to steam-powered vessels. Along the Connecticut and the adjacent waters of the sound, steamships became the important carriers of both people and cargo. Sailing vessels were pulled up into the shallows and allowed to rot away, although some were used in their final days as bulk carriers, bringing coal to markets upstream or carrying quarry stone from Selden Island, Pilgrim's Landing, the Salmon River, and Middle Haddam to construction sites in New York City and Albany. Several of these once proud vessels sank in the Connecticut or coastal waters, forlorn remnants from another time. Today, their cargo can be pushed up on shore by the steady action of the waves and occasionally becomes a beachcomber's prize.

The 20th century: Small town life and the advent of tourism

Although the lower Connecticut River valley was more than adequately served by railroad and trolley systems in the late 19th century, river and shore towns like Lyme, Old Lyme, Essex, and Saybrook did not develop commercially. Shore cities like Bridgeport and New Haven and interior cities like Hartford and Waterbury had become major manufacturing centers. Along the lower river, commercial enterprises were predominantly small and of a localized nature. As a result, these towns developed a decidedly small-town and even rural character. There were a few exceptions, of course. Ivoryton, Deep River, Haddam, and Moodus were in some respects company towns, home to larger "paternalistic" companies that employed immigrant labor and took care of all their workers' needs.

While the rest of the state and the country seemed to be moving headlong into the industrialism and urban growth of the 20th century, the lower river communities maintained an economically low profile. But modern urban life proved to be stressful, and often downright unhealthy. Soon, the idea of "getting away from it all" became popular. One of the places where people went to get away from it all was the lower Connecticut Valley. Resort areas, with cottages and hotels to accommodate the weekend refugees, sprang up in South Lyme, Fenwick, East Haddam, and elsewhere along the river and the sound. Along with resorts, places where tourists could go for concerts or to see a play or look at fine art became part of the lower valley landscape. A popular retreat for artists, Old Lyme became known as the birthplace of American Impressionism. Ironically, it was the summer holiday movement that resulted in most of the development in the once sleepy and rural lower valley region. Indeed, tourism continues to define the region today.

Tidewater marshes of
the lower Connecticut River
adapted from Nels Barrett

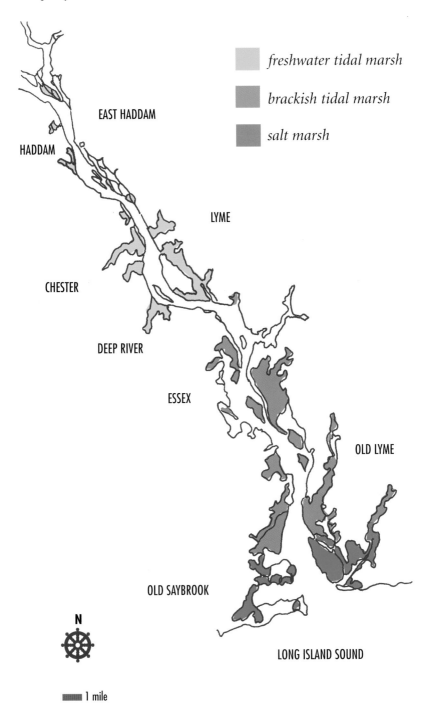

freshwater tidal marsh

brackish tidal marsh

salt marsh

EAST HADDAM

HADDAM

LYME

CHESTER

DEEP RIVER

ESSEX

OLD LYME

OLD SAYBROOK

N

LONG ISLAND SOUND

1 mile

Chapter 3
Tidal Wetland Vegetation

Juliana Panos Barrett and Nels Barrett

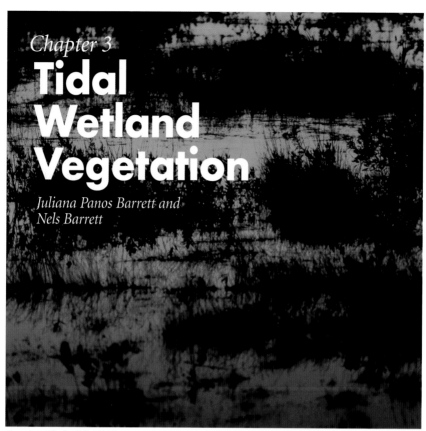

Sunset at Black Hall, Old Lyme

Photo Courtesy of © Robert Benson

Tidal wetlands are special habitats. They are natural gardens supporting an incredible diversity of plant life. Many of these plants are uncommon and unique to tidal wetland environments. Tidal wetlands abound in all low-lying areas within the reach of the flooding tides. The most exemplary tidal wetlands are located downriver from Middletown. Shallow coves and drowned valleys of tributaries carved into bedrock, narrow margins of many small islands, spiraling shores of sandbars, and quiet backwater embayments are occupied by a rich variety of tidal wetland vegetation.

Such astounding diversity of plant life is attributed to factors including changes in the height of the tides, the degree of mixing between fresh and salt waters, and periodic flood disturbances. During the flood tide (high tide), saltwater from Long Island Sound intrudes upriver as a wedge beneath the lighter freshwater of the river, forcibly reversing the current and causing tidal flooding along the river's shores and into the tidal wetlands. At ebb tide (low tide), the saltwater wedge is withdrawn, the water level subsides, and the river resumes its flow back to Long Island Sound. Although mixing between the saltwater of the sound and the freshwater of the river is limited to the Tidewaters region, tidal effects extend considerably farther upriver than the saltwater front.

These unique conditions create a sequence of three intergrading classes of tidal wetlands: (1) salt tidal wetlands, (2) brackish tidal wetlands, and (3) freshwater tidal wetlands. Each of these tidal wetlands is distinguished by a different mixture of plants that grow there. Within each site, slight changes in elevation, ranging from open water to the upland border, dramatically affect which species grow. Various mixtures of plants result in conspicuous vegetation patterns. Separate profiles of the three different tidal wetland types and their unique botanical makeup are described in the sections that follow.

Salt tidal wetlands

Salt tidal wetlands are limited to the coastal area at the mouth of the Connecticut River, extending only about two and one-half miles upriver from Saybrook Jetty (Old Saybrook), including the lower reaches of the Black Hall River (Old Lyme). Within this lowest reach, the salinity (a measure indicating the amount of salt in solution) ranges from about 10 to 30 parts of salt per 1,000 parts of water (parts per thousand or ppt). The height of the tides averages just over 3 feet at the mouth of the Connecticut River. The variety of plants found growing are limited by salinity and how frequently and deeply the plants are immersed by the tides. A belted pattern of vegetation is very evident, progressing from open water to the upland.

Shallow, open waters and flats, when exposed, are often lacking in vegetation. However, algae and aquatic plants typical of coastal embayments

River vegetation

are found growing together in "aquatic beds." Common algae include sea lettuce and green-threads. Other plants found growing in the salt coves and creeks are widgeon grass and horned pondweed.

At the water's edge, where flats, bayfront shores, and creeks are flooded twice daily by tides, there is a zone of salt marsh commonly called the "low marsh." Smooth cord grass is the dominant plant growing from approximately mean sea level to mean high water south of the railroad bridge.

Progressing landward and in areas flooded less often is a zone known as the "high marsh." Above the reach of mean high tide, the high marsh is often dominated by salt meadow hay with other plants in abundance, such as spike grass and black grass. Also growing among the grasses and rushes are other salt marsh plants, e.g. seaside goldenrod, salt marsh aster, salt marsh fleabane, and salt marsh sand-spurrey. Within the high marsh are

disturbed sites, depressions, and low-lying areas called *pannes* where slight changes in marsh elevation cause tidal floodwaters to become trapped. As the saltwater in these *pannes* evaporates, salinity levels can become quite high. Plants common to these extreme sites include glasswort and a short variant of smooth cord grass. Other common plants that may grow within the *pannes* are sea lavender, salt marsh plantain, and seaside gerardia.

To eliminate standing water in the deeper *pannes*, networks of linear, parallel ditches were excavated in nearly all of Connecticut's salt marshes during the early 1930s in an attempt to eradicate mosquitoes. Slight changes in

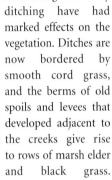

relief brought about by ditching have had marked effects on the vegetation. Ditches are now bordered by smooth cord grass, and the berms of old spoils and levees that developed adjacent to the creeks give rise to rows of marsh elder and black grass. The practice of ditching marshes has been replaced by open water marsh management, a more ecologically sound method of mosquito control that mimics natural conditions. Great Island in Old Lyme is an exemplary saline high marsh. (This particular site was dedicated as "The Dr. Roger Tory Peterson Wildlife Area" in July 2000 to honor the renowned ornithologist who lived in the Tidewaters region for 40 years.)

Still farther landward, at the reach of only the highest of tides and the occasional flood of surging storms, a narrow belt of vegetation forms at the upper border of the salt marsh and edge of the uplands. The vegetation growing here can be quite variable. Shrub thickets of marsh elder and groundsel tree, tall grasslands of switchgrass, or dense colonies of common reed commonly form an upper border. Where groundwater from upland sources is discharged, the freshwater influences the vegetation and additional species are often

Marsh vegetation at high tide, Whalebone Cove, Lyme

Photo Courtesy of © Robert Benson

present, including common three-square, poison ivy, and other wetland plants common to less saline tidal wetlands described in the sections ahead. Examples are found bordering uplands throughout the area.

Brackish tidal wetlands

Brackish tidal wetlands occur in the middle reaches of the lower Connecticut where the salinity averages 10 parts per thousand. Within the brackish zone, the height of the tides averages about 29 inches. The reach of brackish tidal waters spans from just below the railroad bridge between Old Saybrook and Old Lyme north to the town line separating Deep River and Essex. Although the brackish reaches constitute a broad transitional saltwater and freshwater, the wetland plants

Marsh vegetation at low tide

are still limited by salinity and the range of tidal flooding. The zonal appearance of the brackish tidal wetland vegetation beyond the river's shores and creeks takes on more of a mosaic pattern

In brackish waters of the Connecticut River, shallow open waters of creeks and coves support an abundance of aquatic plants. Several of the more typical plants growing in brackish aquatic beds are tapegrass, widgeon grass, and horned pondweed. In less saline waters, ditch moss and sago pondweed grow. The quiet backwaters and flats of Lord Cove (Lyme) are the best examples of brackish aquatic beds.

The regularly flooded brackish low marsh may include a variety of plants more commonly seen in the salt marsh, like smooth cord grass and salt marsh bulrush. Other plants appearing along the shoreline include three-square, estuarine bulrush, and spike-rush. Beneath the canopy of these larger plants, a close inspection reveals many other small plants. These diminutive plants include the spike-rush and eastern lilaeopsis. Good examples include the protected shores of Calves Island and Goose Island (Old Lyme), Lord Cove, Nott Island (Lyme), and Great Meadow (Essex).

At tidal elevations above mean high water, the two major kinds of vegetation include brackish tidal meadows and brackish tidal marshes. Brackish tidal meadows occur commonly behind the bordering marshes and levees where evaporation of infrequent high tides may increase the salinity. Where salt meadow hay dominates, the brackish meadow appears very much like the salt tidal high marsh. In fact, many of the same forbs (non-grass herbaceous plants) found in the salt marsh are actually more predominant in the brackish meadow, including seaside goldenrod, salt marsh aster, arrow grass, salt marsh plantain, and salt marsh fleabane. As other plants are encountered, however, the similarity ends. Other common plants include creeping bent, redtop, a sedge, silverweed, water pimpernel, orach, and switchgrass. Well-developed brackish meadows are found along Ragged Rock Creek and Ferry Point (Old Saybrook) and on Upper Island and Calves Island (Old Lyme).

Brackish tidal marshes are recognized by large and impressive stands of either cattails or the common reed. As friends of the Connecticut River know all too well, *Phragmites* (common reed) is rapidly displacing many of the native plants here. Restoration efforts by the Connecticut Department of Environmental Protection, The Nature Conservancy, Connecticut College, and local land trusts are under way in several nearby areas. Farther upriver, these brackish marshes may grade imperceptibly into freshwater counterparts with the same dominant species. However, common cattail is the more common dominant of freshwater tidal marshes. Other brackish marsh species commonly found here include rose mallow, switch grass, and climbing hempweed. Big cord grass is often found on brackish creek levees. The vegetation at the upland border of the brackish marsh varies depending upon the amount of freshwater influence. Phragmites and poison ivy are common. Examples of brackish marshes are found along the lower section of Lieutenant River, Goose Island (Old Lyme), Lord Cove, Nott Island, and Great Meadow.

Freshwater tidal wetlands

Freshwater tidal wetlands occur beyond the reach of the tidal salt front. Like other tidal wetlands, they are still affected by the flooding of the tides. Freshwater tidal wetlands are best developed where changes in the heights of the tides exceed one and one-half feet. At tidal ranges below that, the wetland vegetation becomes less distinguishable from lower floodplain vegetation, except for a very narrow zone along the shore. The height of the tides gradually diminishes up the Connecticut River, dropping below the one-and one-half-foot threshold at Botkin Rock in Middletown. The most exemplary freshwater tidal wetlands are distributed along the Connecticut River from Deep River to the East Haddam bridge approximately 16 miles upriver. In spite of the strong influence of tidal flooding, the vegetation of freshwater tidal wetlands is not as distinctly zoned as that of the other tidal wetlands. Instead, the vegetation pattern appears as an interesting mosaic of patches. The patchwork of vegetation results largely from the suitability of the freshwater tidal habitat to support a large collection of plants. Most of the plants encountered here grow elsewhere in nontidal wetlands. Select groups of plants, however, will grow only here.

The freshwater subtidal habitat is not unlike ordinary ponds. A large variety of floating and submersed plants occurs often as a mix of several plants in an aquatic bed. Floating leaves and striking flowers of yellow pond lilies and water lilies grace the surface of quiet tidal waters. Submersed

Flowering *Phragmites* along the Connecticut River

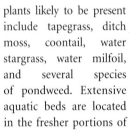

plants likely to be present include tapegrass, ditch moss, coontail, water stargrass, water milfoil, and several species of pondweed. Extensive aquatic beds are located in the fresher portions of Lord Cove (Lyme), Selden Cove(Lyme), and Chapman Pond (East Haddam).

Wild rice is a tall annual grass that is most conspicuous in late summer. Most often it grows by itself along sandy river shores and tidal flats that are only infrequently exposed at elevations below the mean tidal level. The best stands of wild rice are found on the flats behind Eustasia Island (Deep River), Whalebone Creek (Hadlyme), and in the quiet backwaters of Post Cove and Pratt Cove (Deep River).

More readily exposed tidal flats and shores between mean tide level and mean high tide are populated by many types of robust broad-leaved emergent plants, including several kinds of arrowleaf. Other similar plants growing here are pickerelweed and arrow-arum, arrowhead, and extensive stands of the aromatic sweetflag. Less common plants include two kinds of bur-marigolds, spike-rushes, and bulrushes. The best

places to find these emergent plants are the flats and shores of Selden Cove (Lyme). Many of these are found along muddy creek banks throughout the freshwater tidal reaches, like Chester Creek (Chester) and Selden Creek (Lyme).

Gravelly tidal shores along the many tidal tributaries that join the Connecticut River are sparsely vegetated between mean tide level and mean high tide. The plants that do manage to grow on intermittently exposed gravel flats include many diminutive plants like marsh purslane, false pimpernel, golden-pert, pipeworts, pygmyweed, and mud purslane. Above mean high tide, the more stable conditions allow a much broader diversity of species. These include waterpepper, smartweeds, small-flowered St. Johnswort, marsh St. Johnswort, purple loosestrife, seedbox, boneset, germander, cardinal flower, beggar's tick, common sneezeweed, rattlesnake grass, and Japanese stilt grass. Good examples of gravelly shores occur along the Eightmile River (Lyme), the upper reaches of Deep River, and Mile Creek (Lyme).

Chapter
Birds
Noble Proctor

Connecticut River bald eagle

Courtesy of Frank Gallo

The bird life of the lower Connecticut River has been studied closely for over 150 years. In 1843, Linsley talked of the "richness of bird life" at the mouth of the Connecticut River, as did Merriam in his 1877 publication, *A Review of the Birds of Connecticut*. The lower Connecticut River is really a window on the bird populations of the state. But the river environment has changed, not only physically, with the dramatic alterations of sites like Griswold Point, but also biologically, with the invasion of *Phragmites*.

The last 50 years have also seen the bird populations fluctuate dramatically. Willets,

for instance, used to nest in the lower river marshlands in the late 1800s, before disappearing for nearly 100 years. A recent reinvasion, however, has made them a common nester today. In 1942, a massive immigration of snowy egrets from the south started a yearly pattern that now makes them a common sight of the summer and fall marshland environment. The coves and marshes described in this book provide wonderful habitat for an exemplary bird community.

Birding the lower river: Winter

Each season brings its own special highlight, and a visit to one of the many birding areas of the lower river is sure to yield interesting and exciting finds. Winter, for example, is the best time of year to see bald eagles. Over the years, we have seen more and more eagles returning to an area of concentration that starts at the Salmon River boat launch and extends down to the islands off Essex and the open stretches of Great Island. A stop at any spot in between is sure to reward you with a sighting. Sometimes, you might even see several eagles in the winter skies since as many as fifty have been counted here in recent years.

While watching for eagles, you will no doubt notice other birds of prey that winter in the lower river area such as northern harriers, rough-legged hawks, red-tailed hawks, red-shouldered hawks, and even a rarity like a golden eagle. Large groups of ducks also populate the winter river and dock areas, including flocks of gleaming white common mergansers with green heads and red bills, groups of bufflehead

Great blue heron

Courtesy of Frank Gallo

bobbing along like corks, and the common goldeneye with a distinct white spot between its eye and bill. A haven for ducks, the coves provide abundant food in the form of small crustaceans and submerged vegetation.

At the mouth of the river look out for common loons, a common winter resident. Some of the loons may nest in the Connecticut Lakes area—the origin of the river. Occasionally, red-throated loons or red-necked grebes, rare species of gull or northern gannets can be spotted at the mouth of the river. Essentially, the mouth of the river provides high quality habitats for more northern species to spend the winter and prepare for another nesting season.

Spring birding

With the arrival of spring, migrant birds appear in the wooded corridors along the river's edge, while marsh birds move into cattail pockets to breed. Early February sees the arrival of the first red-winged blackbirds, which will advertise and defend their well-established territories by March. By the end of the first week in April, tree swallows appear, as do the first clapper rails. The rails arrive by night and are always difficult to observe; however, their distinct clacking call gives away their presence. They are some of the more common birds of the salt and brackish marshes. Great Island and the other salt marshes at the mouth of the river provide the lower river's only habitats for two species of sparrow, the salt marsh sharp-tailed sparrow and the seaside sparrow.

By late April the "flood" of migrants begins. Yellow warblers, hooded warblers, orioles, and marsh wrens move in the woodedge and marsh, while shorebirds dot the mudflats to feed during their journey north. At low tide, wherever mud is exposed, scan for these travelers. Over 30 species of shorebirds have been recorded on the lower river during migration. These long distance migrants depend on extensive mudflats as critical stopover points on their migrations. Among the more common shorebirds are semipalmated sandpipers, black-bellied plovers, greater yellowlegs, short-billed dowitchers, and dunlins. On the outer shores, spectacular oystercatchers with bright orange bills and black and white bodies have happily become a common sight (they were very rare only 20 years ago). During storms in late April and early May, head to the shore and scan for gannets that have been blown into Long Island Sound by nor'easters. These huge birds with brilliant white plumage and black wing tips put on a spectacular show as they plunge for food at the mouth of the river.

Summer and the birding is easy
When the common and least terns arrive, we know that summer is not far behind. Along the lower river, there are many species of birds to be found during the summer. The osprey, for instance, is as

Great egret in a patch of wild rice

Courtesy of The Nature Conservancy

much a symbol of the lower Connecticut River in the summer as any bird. Another summer bird is the willet, with its bold zebra-striped wings and raucous *pill-will-willet* calls. Dotting the marshes' edges all along the lower river are both great and snowy egrets foraging for food to take back to their nestlings on Fisher's Island.

Other long-legged waders include the great blue herons that have not gone inland to nest and green herons, common breeders in the trees all along the river's edge.

Marsh wrens that arrived in spring are now breeding in earnest. Singing from the tops of cattails and reeds, the male constructs up to ten ball-shaped nests, but the female will use only one. The remaining nests are built to confuse predators searching for eggs. You can also hear sharp-tailed sparrows (which share the multiple nest strategy) and seaside sparrows singing their insect-like buzzing songs and watch them as they skim low over the salt marsh grasses. Just a reminder: summer is nesting time, so birds may be more difficult to see and caution must be taken not to disturb nesting sites.

Listen too for the loud rattling calls of belted kingfishers which nest in earthen banks along the river. Song sparrows, common grackles and common yellowthroats have also "set up shop" for the summer. The yellowthroat's *witchety, witchety, witchety* song becomes one of the most common songs in the freshwater marshes. Heard but not seen will be rails and bitterns such as Virginia rail and American bittern, two species that are the subject of monitoring due to the loss of wetland habitats throughout Connecticut. The freshwater tidal marshes of the lower Connecticut represent some of the best habitats in the state for marsh birds.

Semipalmated sandpiper and plovers

Courtesy of Frank Gallo

Autumn splendors

Fall begins early on the river. Tree swallows start to form flocks by the first week in August, and shorebirds are already returning from nesting in the high Arctic. The shortening days of September mean that fall migration is well under way as the great exodus south continues. Warblers are now decked out in drab fall plumage as a protection against the hawks that are also migrating. Finding warblers in a wooded spot on the riverbanks can be a challenge, but also great fun. Very often, warblers move with vireos, thrushes, and sparrows and are, in turn, joined by chickadees, titmice, and nuthatches. They join forces for the advantage of searching for insects in flocks, which are more successful than birds searching individually—and to benefit from the safety that comes with traveling in numbers.

Coves such as Selden Creek or Pratt Cove with abundant fruiting shrubs and wild rice provide superb feeding habitats for these migrating flocks. Hundreds of blackbirds, sora rails, and mixed flocks of songbirds will be present to store up fuel to continue their fall migration or to prepare for the colder months ahead. Many species of ducks attracted by the quiet waters and abundant food in turn attract hunters into the coves in October.

Birds of prey are always a fall spectacle. On the coast, hundreds of sharp-shinned hawks and kestrels, along with scattered harriers, Cooper's hawks, and migrant osprey, provide exciting birding. A highlight is spotting a peregrine falcon as it skims over the marsh or along the beach with arrow-like speed. Fortunately, this species is well on the way to recovery in eastern North America. In the evening, if you scan low over the meadows, try to spot a short-eared owl as it sets out for an evening hunt.

The coves, marshes and open waters of the river provide excellent habitats for numerous birds, but these habitats are changing. As noted in the introduction, common reed or *Phragmites* is taking over many of the marshes. It is widely held that wildlife habitat is greatly improved by eradicating dense stands of *Phragmites*, allowing a number of native species to grow providing food and cover for many species. The only wildlife use of *Phragmites* of note is for limited nesting of *red wing* blackbirds and marsh wrens and as roosting sites for common grackles, red-winged blackbirds and tree swallows. In one location more than 1 million tree swallows use a *Phragmites* stand for a roost during fall migration. Such a unique phenomenon merits protection for this particular site, but in general, the health of the river edge and marshes requires management of this invasive plant.

Birding the lower Connecticut River is time well spent no matter what the season. The more exploring you do, the more you will understand why so many people believe the lower Connecticut River is one of the richest bird life areas in the state.

The Osprey Project

Perhaps the greatest success in aiding a species in trouble has been the Osprey Project, which began nearly 50 years ago. In the late 1950's, only a few of these magnificent birds nested at the river's mouth. Struggling from the effects of the pesticide DDT, the population seemed doomed. Roger Tory Peterson, ornithologist and author of *A Field Guide to the Birds*, made the public aware of what was happening by traveling to Washington to call attention to their plight. Scientific studies showed that eggshells were thinned by the presence of DDT in the birds' diet. DDT was finally banned and protective steps were taken. Management included egg exchanges from healthy populations and the foster-parenting of young brought to the nests. A nesting platform program was also instituted, since osprey nest sites were being lost to coastal storms. The Osprey Project was a great success and is tended yearly by dedicated volunteers who assure it's continued success. The remarkable recuperative powers of this species are evidenced by the greater than 20 pairs of ospreys that nest and produce young at the mouth of the river each year.

Another area of success is Griswold Point, which has become a nesting refuge for the federally endangered piping plover

Osprey nest

as well as the diminutive and threatened least tern. The Nature Conservancy owns Griswold Point and employs a preserve steward to protect the plovers and terns and educate the public about their conservation. These stewards have a wealth of information and are eager to share it.

Shorebird stopover habitats

The mudflats around Griswold Point, Great Island and the Lieutenant and Blackhall river marshes provide vital stopover habitats for migrating shorebirds. The birds often fly for thousands of miles at a time and rely on these habitats to rest and feed to continue their journey. The thousands of birds that use the river are feeding on the rich invertebrate community in the mudflats and are trying to store fat for their long flights ahead. Some go as far as southern South America. It is important to observe these birds from a distance and not frighten them by walking through flocks or boating too close.

Mute swans

One of the other success stories on the river comes with a price. Non-native mute swans were first introduced to this country in the 19th century. The species has expanded its range throughout the eastern seaboard and, in the lower Connecticut, has become a nuisance species. These 20-pound birds have a voracious diet of vegetation and are diminishing the abundance of food for wintering waterfowl. The Connecticut Department of Environmental Protection recommends an egg-addling program to limit mute swan populations. Boaters beware, nesting mute swans are highly aggressive and can be quite dangerous.

Chapter 5
Fishes

Stephen Gephard

Top: American shad, bottom: Atlantic salmon

Courtesy of The Nature Conservancy, S.Gephard

ome people believe that all fish really need is water. As long as the water is clean and fit, a fish will flourish. Maybe that's true for pet fish in an aquarium, but in natural waters, fish need more than just water. They need habitat. Habitat provides them with the essentials for life and defines what fish live where. The coves, creeks, marshes, and backwaters of the lower Connecticut River are fish habitat—excellent habitat. Ironically, some of the components to a good habitat may be what small boat explorers can't stand: low, overhanging branches; clogging growth of submerged aquatic vegetation; washed-out gravel banks; curving, serpentine channels; propeller-eating snags and boulders; and discreet channels that break up into a labyrinth of quickly shrinking threads of open water.

Mainstream and cove/inlet habitats

The habitats provided by the mainstream river and the various coves and inlets are very different. The "big-water" and often deep water habitat of the mainstream river is important to many adult fish, although the strong water velocities and lack of cover make it inhospitable to other fishes at

various times of the year. Taken together, the mainstream river and the coves provide fishes with all they need in the Connecticut River ecosystem.

A major distinction between the main stem and the coves and inlets is the stability of the habitat. The underwater habitat of the main river is dynamic, but the river is so big that the number of various habitat types remains, over time, about the same. For instance, a sandbar in Haddam may wash away in a flood, but the storm might create a new sandbar downriver in Chester, so over time there is little change. Consequently, the river's appearance is quite similar to what it was in the 1600s, while the habitat and general appearance of the coves and tributaries can change dramatically. When settlers first arrived in the area, Whalebone Creek was reported to have a deepwater habitat suitable for anchoring ships. Now, the creek is a shallow marsh. Chapman Pond likewise looks considerably different than it did in 1950, much less 1750.

Fish spawning

Because coves and tributary inlets, creeks, and marshes are all different, they offer a variety of habitats for a number of fish species. The marshes that have built up in the streamway or floodplain of the river (e.g., Ragged Rock Creek, Lord Cove, Pratt and Post creeks, Selden Creek) are mostly backwaters that are dominated by Connecticut River water. They are used extensively as spawning and nursery areas by fish looking for a spot away from the strong current. The presence of some of the fish may be due to chance rather than deliberate strategy. If you see a white perch in Selden Creek, that fish probably did not specifically seek out Selden Creek, but rather was in the Connecticut River and sought a lower-velocity area and just happened upon Selden Creek. It could have just as easily entered Chapman Pond or Whalebone Creek.

The lower river coves and inlets are essential for spawning. Few species spawn in the main stem of the lower Connecticut River because the streambed can easily shift and bury deposited eggs. Eggs could also be swept away by flows and transported into saltwater (which the eggs of most freshwater and anadromous species cannot tolerate). The coves and inlets of the lower river are full of juvenile fish feeding on the abundant resources of the shallow water. There are predators in these areas, to be sure, including kingfishers, herons, and egrets, as well as larger fish. Extensive cover and diminished water currents not present in the mainstream river, however, provide some protection. Small perch, bass, and pike may spend their first year or so in one of these shallow inlets.

Winter refuge

The coves and marshes also provide winter refuge. Fish are cold-blooded creatures, and their metabolism and energy output slow down in cold temperatures. A lethargic largemouth bass would have great difficulty maintaining its position in the mainstream river during winter, particularly in March when freshets accelerate water velocity. Typically, many species of fish (bass, catfishes, sunfishes, perch) begin occupying the various tributary coves and creeks in October and November when temperatures begin to drop. They will stay there until the spring freshet is over and temperatures begin to rise. It is for this reason that commercial fishing is prohibited in many of the coves.

Saltwater visitors

Some of the fishes found in the backwaters of the lower Connecticut River are saltwater species, visitors from the oceans. Some, like the bluefish, venture in a short distance, usually on feeding forays. Others, like adult menhaden, are trying to escape predators on feeding forays; still others like crevalle jacks, seahorses, and needlefish, feed and grow in the river.

Some saltwater fishes need the river for some part of their life cycle, such as winter flounders that spawn below the Baldwin Bridge or hogchokers that use the entire lower river as a nursery. These marine species are most often found downstream of Hamburg Cove and often in the salty marshes of Old Lyme and Old Saybrook.

Freshwater residents

The fishes we most often encounter in the lower Connecticut are freshwater residents. Their entire life cycle takes place in the river, including, at some point, the marshes and coves. They may not be common south of Hamburg Cove (although don't be surprised if you catch a catfish in the coves of Essex), but they are ubiquitous in all the other coves and marshes of the lower river. Some are native (yellow perch, pumpkinseed, white sucker, spottail shiner, banded killifish, chain pickerel, brown bullhead) and many have been introduced from other regions in the past and have naturalized (largemouth bass, smallmouth bass, bluegill, northern pike, channel catfish, and white catfish). The carp was actually introduced from Europe.

The distributions of fishes in the various coves and marshes can be predicted with some accuracy. Yellow perch are in Whalebone Creek, pumpkinseeds are in Joshua Creek, white perch are in Hamburg Cove, banded killifish are in Selden Creek, carp spawn in Chapman Pond in June, white suckers are in Salmon Cove. But the fact is, any of these fish could be found in any of the inlets.

Finally, there are the diadromous fishes, the species that migrate back and forth

Spring fishing on the Lieutenant River

between the river and saltwater. Most of them are anadromous, meaning that they hatch in freshwater and stay there for some period of a juvenile phase, then migrate to the ocean to feed and grow to adulthood, only to migrate back to the freshwater area of their origin and spawn as mature adults.

Herring, shad, alewives

The Connecticut River has some of the largest anadromous fish runs in the Northeast, and the marshes, coves, and tributaries contribute to this abundance. Alewives, for instance, spawn in most of the inlets covered by this guide. Notable spring runs take place in the Lieutenant River (and Mill Brook), Hamburg Cove (and Eightmile River), Chester Creek, and Chapman Pond. Often, they are blocked by the first dam on the stream, although fishways at these dams would allow them to continue farther upstream, eventually increasing the size of the run. Fishways are currently in place on Mill Brook, Eightmile River, Joshua Creek, and Salmon River. The Connecticut Department of Environmental Protection, Connecticut River Watershed Council, and Conte Refuge are actively working with dam owners to provide access to historic spawning areas.

Blueback herring are similar to alewives, but they favor slightly larger streams. Notable runs take place in the Eightmile, Salmon, and Coginchaug rivers. American shad are actually large herring, and they spawn mostly in the mainstream river north of Hartford, although small numbers ascend the Mattabasett and Salmon rivers (a restoration attempt is under way for the Eightmile River). Juvenile alewives, blueback herring, and shad are found in all the coves and inlets of the lower river. To best appreciate them, paddle from Chapman Pond to Selden Creek (in and out of the coves) around dusk in August and early September. The young fish will be "popping" at the water surface by the thousands as they feed on hatching insects.

Sea lamprey and sea-run browns

Sea lamprey are found in most streams, and notable runs take place in the Eightmile and Salmon rivers and in Roaring and Pattaconk brooks. One can look for their trench-like nests in rapid streams above the head-of-tide in late June. White perch are found everywhere—some are anadromous, while others are freshwater residents. Brown trout are native to Europe, but have naturalized here due to extensive hatchery stockings. Some of them develop an anadromous lifestyle similar to salmon and are referred to as "sea-run" brown trout. They tend to be more silvery than freshwater trout and may reach up to 10 pounds in weight. The sea-run browns are commonly found in the Eightmile and Salmon rivers and in Whalebone and Higganum creeks. But don't bother looking for them; they are solitary and secretive.

Striped bass, sturgeon, and the ubiquitous eel

Striped bass are abundant in the mainstream river, and less common in the backwaters. They are, however, regularly found in Salmon and Hamburg coves during the spring. Similarly, sturgeon and hickory shad rarely venture out of the main stem, although hickory shad are commonly found around Griswold Point and Great Island in the fall. Rainbow smelt that spawn in tributaries during the late winter still remain somewhat a mystery. Federally endangered shortnosed sturgeon are found in this area of the river. Finally, there's the American eel. What can be said about the eel, other than that it is catadromous (it spawns in the oceans and grows to adulthood in freshwater) and is found virtually everywhere. There is not a single place mentioned in this guide where one can't find eels.

Pressures of development

The coves and backwater marshes of the lower Connecticut have always been prized by boaters for their scenic beauty. However, there has been and will continue to be strong development pressures on most of these inlet areas. People who want to live on and near them usually want to build a dock to house a boat considerably larger than the waters can support. Proposals to dredge, fill, remove tilting trees, yank snags, and straighten curves soon follow. If these actions are allowed, the lower Connecticut River may soon begin to resemble the estuaries near New York City, where fish no longer run in significant numbers. We will have, in effect, performed a lobotomy on our river, and fish will be forced to live in a habitat that's stripped of its value.

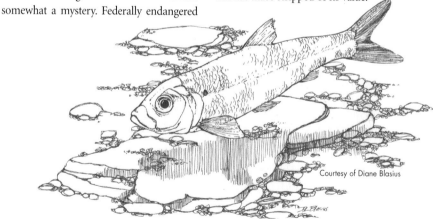

Courtesy of Diane Blasius

Chapter 6

River Fauna

Geoffrey A. Hammerson

Monarch butterflies on goldenrod at Griswold Point   Courtesy of Hank Golet

The tidal waters of the Connecticut River support a rich diversity of animal life. Some members of our river fauna are staggeringly abundant, whereas others are rare and seldom observed. The animals you might see from your boat or from shore vary considerably, depending on such factors as water salinity and temperature, current, tide, the type of vegetation that is present, substrate conditions (for example, muddy, sandy, or rocky), and the time of year. Additionally, ecosystems are ever changing, so what you find here today may be gone tomorrow, and tomorrow may bring something new. Preceding chapters in this book have discussed the birds and fishes of the lower river. The following is a selected overview of the "other 90 percent" of the fauna of the tidal portion of the Connecticut River and its coves.

Mammals

Wild mammals tend to be secretive or nocturnal, and so while they may be common in the lower river valley, most are not often seen. Grass-eating meadow voles are well hidden in their runways in high salt marshes and other riverside areas having thick grass. Star-nosed moles, resembling something out of Dr. Seuss, are common though seldom observed burrowing and semiaquatic mammals of the river's freshwater wetlands, where they seek worms and various aquatic invertebrates. White-tailed deer quietly visit the river and cove edges to forage on wetland plants that provide them with important sources of sodium.

Raccoons are familiar riverside foragers, while minks and muskrats range throughout the tidal river's edges and marshes. The rarely seen but fairly common mink preys on the muskrat and other aquatic animals; the more numerous muskrat feeds primarily on the succulent parts of cattails and other marsh plants and sometimes on river mussels. Hungry harbor seals in search of fish occasionally make brief sojourns up the river during their winter/spring residency in Long Island Sound. River otters also prey on fish and other aquatic animals, but they are scarce in the lower river and its coves. At dusk in the warmer months, bats of several species come to the river to drink and feast on moths, beetles, flies, and other small flying insects.

Many of the lower river mammals leave signs of their presence. Chief among these is the beaver. Along some parts of the tidal freshwater portion of the river, beavers leave felled cottonwoods, willows, and other trees as evidence of their residency. Sometimes they dam small river tributaries near their stream bank dens. The beaver's tree cutting and dam building activities can result in profound changes in the river tributary ecosystems.

Reptiles

Typical reptiles of the freshwater tidal ecosystem include the snapping turtle, painted turtle, and northern water snake. All three are more abundant in the coves and productive marshy areas connected to the river than in the river proper. Both turtles, which feed on various small animals and plants, also inhabit brackish river marshes. A modest population of diamondback terrapins can be found in the salt marshes and tidal channels near the mouth of the river, supported by rich populations of crustaceans and mollusks. There are no venomous snakes along the river, although the fish- and frog-eating water snake is often mistaken for one. Reptiles are active primarily in spring and summer and spend the winter burrowed in the mud, like turtles, or underground in upland sites near water, like water snakes.

Amphibians

Although amphibians are intolerant of saltwater and are therefore absent from the lowest portion of the river and its marshes, several frogs and toads breed in freshwater coves (never in the river itself). American toads, spring peepers, gray treefrogs, green frogs, and pickerel frogs can be heard singing in some of the coves in spring, followed by summer-breeding bullfrogs. The northern leopard frog is restricted in central Connecticut to floodplain wetlands and meadows, especially along the Connecticut River. In some locations, large numbers of wood frogs breed in vernal pools near the river, but these frogs are not part of the typical river-cove amphibian fauna. The bullfrog and pickerel frog can breed successfully in water containing predatory fishes, but the other species rely on fish-free water for larval growth and survival.

The only salamander in the lower Connecticut River is the mudpuppy, a powerful predatory species that grows up to a foot in length. Whether it's a native or introduced species is debatable. This gilled amphibian is found in the northernmost edge of the tidal Connecticut River and feeds on various aquatic invertebrates. Like reptiles, amphibians here are active primarily in the spring and summer and are dormant in winter.

Crustaceans

Many schooling fishes are supported to a large degree by small crustaceans. Populations of speck-like planktonic copepods and cladocerans of several species generally peak in the river in late spring and early summer. They are important as food for many small fishes and the immature stages of larger ones. Saltwater and brackish water habitats are inhabited by vast numbers of amphipods, isopods, shore shrimps, sand shrimps, fiddler crabs, green crabs (introduced), and blue crabs. Most of these, in turn, are nourished by microscopic phytoplankton, algae, and microorganisms attached to rocks and shells or growing on the surface of marsh peat and mud, carrion, or decaying marsh plants. Crustaceans

Snapping turtle, Lord Cove

Courtesy of The Nature Conservancy

are ecologically important in ways independent of their place in the food chain. For example, marsh edges are riddled by small burrows dug by fiddler crabs. The burrows facilitate aeration of the mud where smooth cord grass grows, augmenting the delivery of nutrients and oxygen to the plant roots and greatly enhancing their growth.

A distinct change in the river's crustacean fauna takes place where water salinity changes. For example, the typical fiddler crab in river-mouth salt marshes is the mud fiddler crab or, in sandy sites, the sand fiddler. But in brackish waters and adjacent freshwater upstream, the red-jointed fiddler replaces these. Fiddler and other crabs, as well as marine shrimp, disappear altogether as one moves well into the freshwater zone, but scavenging amphipods, isopods, and ostracods ("seed shrimp") can be numerous. Omnivorous crayfishes also are present.

Some crustaceans, however, tolerate a wide range of salinity. Blue crabs, for example, move seasonally between saltwater and brackish water. The distribution of blue crabs often varies with river flows. In dry years, when the salt wedge moves farther upriver, crabs can be found as far upstream as Haddam. In wet years, when high flows limit the salt wedge, they usually range only as far as Essex. They are common enough in the lower river to support a modest recreational shellfishery.

Barnacles, while most common on the rocky coast of Long Island Sound, sometimes range into and actively feed in the river's brackish water zone as far upstream as Brockway Island, often attached to floating logs that drift with the tides. These crustaceans use feathery appendages to extract plankton and detritus from the water.

Finding blue crabs

Courtesy of Robert Perron

Insects

In spring and summer, you can see in the freshwater lower river, and especially its coves, a wide variety of predatory, scavenging, and herbivorous insect larvae or adults. The list includes mayflies, dragonflies, damselflies, stoneflies, water striders, backswimmers, giant water bugs, water measurers, water scorpions, dobsonflies, caddisflies, diving beetles, water scavenger beetles, crawling water beetles, waterlily leaf beetles, whirligig beetles, water penny beetles, midges, punkies, crane flies, sand flies, and black flies. Shallow waters often support enormous numbers of water boatmen, but in summer some river-cove shallows become remarkably warm (over 100°F) and may be devoid of any insect life.

Beds of water lilies or pickerelweed in quiet freshwater tidal areas support a rich variety of insects. When in bloom, they often attract nectar and pollen feeders such as bumblebees, honeybees, halictid bees, and syrphid flies. These insects also pollinate the flowers of river-edge plants such as buttonbush and basswood. You can tell by the ragged and holey appearance of water lily leaves in summer how important these plants are as animal food. Water lily leaf beetles are ecologically linked with water lilies and other aquatic plants, which furnish the diet of both larvae and adults. The larvae of several moth species—in a radical departure from the usual land-dwelling lifestyle of butterfly and moth caterpillars—are highly aquatic and feed on the leaves of water lilies, pickerelweed, and cattails. After a period of feeding, the caterpillars swim to shore, overwinter in leaf litter, pupate in spring, and eventually emerge as moths. The leaves and spongy leaf stems of water lilies and pickerelweed also provide egg-laying sites for water scorpions, backswimmers, and certain dragonflies such as the common green darner. Attached to the undersurface of water lily leaves you might also find grazing snails and the egg clumps of various invertebrate populations of beetles, damselflies, caddisflies, snails, and water mites. The thick growth of water lily beds also shelters many small fishes.

In the spring, under cover on shore, you might find an interesting insect called a hellgrammite. It's the strong-jawed larval stage of the dobsonfly. After spending a number of years living among stones on the river bottom, these impressive (often more than 3 inches long) aquatic predators crawl ashore to pupate on land.

Flying insects

At various times of the year the flying adult stages of insects with aquatic larvae may fill the air. Particularly abundant are the many species of harmless mosquito-like flies known as midges, massive numbers of which sometimes emerge in early summer. Less abundant, but individually more lively and impressive, are dragonflies and damselflies, regular river companions on any summer boating excursion. Dragonflies and damselflies are predators as aquatic larvae and as flying adults. Larvae live in the water for generally 1-to-3 years before metamorphosing in spring or summer into flying adults, which, in New England, do not survive the winter.

A tramp through a marsh might yield various plant-eating insects, including grasshoppers, ground crickets, various plant-juice-sucking homopteran insects, and beetles. In summer and early fall, the *tick-tick-tick-tick-buzzzzzz* of meadow katydids is a conspicuous and familiar sound. Overall, relatively little of the living marsh plant biomass is consumed by these plant-eating insects or by the herbivorous mammals previously discussed. Much more is cycled into animal populations via decomposers and detritus feeders that consume dead plant material. Two species of introduced mantids (better known as "praying mantis") prey on other marsh insects.

Butterflies

The butterflies you might see along the river include a wide assortment of species, but most are not strictly associated with the plant life of the tidal waters of the river and its coves. The species most often seen while paddling along the river's edge are tiger swallowtails and red admirals. Swallowtail caterpillars feed on the leaves of various streamside trees and shrubs, whereas red admiral larvae subsist on nettles. In July and August, broad-winged skippers perch on common reed, which provides food for its caterpillars. The well-known monarch attracts attention in late summer and early fall as large numbers gather on seaside goldenrods near the river's mouth on their migratory journey to wintering sites in the mountains of central Mexico.

The salt marsh dragonfly

Insect diversity is relatively low in the salty waters at the river's mouth. However, there is one salt marsh insect worthy of note. It's the

A Seaside Dragonlet *(Erythodiplax berenice)*

salt marsh dragonfly, the only strictly salt marsh dragonfly species in all of North America. The predatory adults are a natural control on another, less welcome insect—the salt marsh mosquito. Blood-seeking adult female greenhead flies and deerflies, which develop as larvae in marshes, can be bothersome in summer but, fortunately, seldom are abundant enough to ruin a paddle through the marshes.

Tiger beetles

It's impossible to discuss every insect you might see near the river and its coves, but among the non-aquatic groups that might catch your eye are the tiger beetles. These half-inch-long predators stalk the sandy beaches of the river throughout its tidal portion. Both the adult and burrowing larval stages prey on flies, ants, and other insects. One species, the puritan tiger beetle, is a rarity, restricted to scattered areas along the Connecticut River in Connecticut and Massachusetts and a few places in the Chesapeake Bay region. It is a federally protected endangered species. The adults emerge in early summer after overwintering twice in the larval stage. Predatory robber flies often hunt near active groups of adult tiger beetles, presumably seeking similar prey.

Spiders

Spiders are well represented along the lower Connecticut River, and some exhibit lengthy activity periods that extend well into the colder months. Wolf spiders usually are abundant on the ground and among plants in all marshes. Fishing spiders are common in many freshwater marshes. These large spiders use their legs to row or gallop over the water surface, dive easily under water, and sometimes capture and eat prey as large as small fish and amphibian larvae.

Mollusks

Typical mollusks of the saltwater portion of the Connecticut River ecosystem include mud snails, marsh snails, and ribbed mussels. Mud snails graze on algae, microscopic organisms, and dead animals on subtidal and intertidal mud. These snails have a heavy shell designed to protect them from many potential predators and so, accordingly, are often tremendously abundant. The smaller, more delicate salt marsh snails graze in huge numbers on exposed peat of the high marsh. These air-breathers may perch on grass stems above the water when the marsh is flooded. Ribbed mussels occur in large numbers attached to the base of smooth cord grass growing along tidal channels. They feed on bits of organic matter they filter from the water.

These salt marsh mollusks are replaced in freshwater areas by other species, including several kinds of snails and clams. A careful search of rocks, plants, shells, detritus, wood, or sand or silt bottoms in the tidal Connecticut River might yield a dozen species of native snails, most of which are found in quiet waters. An exotic newcomer, the Chinese mystery snail, may now be established in the river's tidal freshwaters. It grows up to 2 inches long and grazes on shallow, sandy, or muddy bottoms.

Many species of tiny fingernail clams inhabit the bottom in the freshwater section of the river, especially in sandy substrates, but the river mollusks most likely to be noticed are the larger freshwater mussels, including the eastern pondmussel, tidewater mucket, eastern lampmussel, eastern elliptio, triangle floater, and alewife floater. These filter feeders include species that may reach several inches in length. All of them depend on fish to act as hosts for their minute larvae. After being released from the mother mussel, the larvae clamp onto the gills or skin of a fish and live as a parasite for up to several weeks before dropping to the bottom and developing into a typical mussel. The larvae, or glochidia, do little or no harm to the parasitized fish. Two mussels, the dwarf wedgemussel and yellow lampmussel, are now very rare or extirpated in the lower river valley, evidently victims of water pollution. In fact, freshwater mussels are one of the most endangered groups of animals worldwide.

Asiatic clam

Aside from pollution, another potential threat to our native freshwater mussels is the Asiatic clam. This mollusk, which was probably introduced here as discarded fishing bait, became exceedingly abundant during the 1990s, particularly in the vicinity of the Connecticut Yankee nuclear power plant (and in its cooling system as well). The clam's rapid spread evidently resulted from the favorable warm waters discharged by the plant, coupled with the clam's prolific reproduction and effective dispersal mechanism (the clam may be buoyed into the river current by means of a mucous strand that it secretes). The Asiatic clam tends to dominate stream-bottom habitats, but it is a warm-water mollusk. Winter temperatures may prevent the Asiatic clam from displacing native species here in Connecticut. It will be interesting to see what happens to the population now that the power plant is no longer operational.

Zebra mussel

River ecologists have been wary for the appearance of the zebra mussel, a European native that has become established elsewhere in the United States (and in at least one lake in Connecticut). This dark and light banded clam, usually an inch long as an adult, has the capacity to form dense aggregations that can overwhelm native mussels and damage aquatic ecosystems through their enormous water-filtering capacity.

Other invertebrates

One of the most surprising invertebrates of the river's tidal freshwaters is the giant bryozoan. You can recognize this colonial animal by its somewhat brainlike appearance. It consists of rosettes of reddish zooids embedded in gelatinous material (secreted by the zooids), usually found growing in shaded, quiet waters. It increases in size throughout the warmer months and, attached to submerged logs, may grow to several feet across. Colonies disintegrate as water temperatures drop in early fall. The bryozoan survives winter as a resistant flattened seedlike structure that germinates into a zooid in spring. Colonies form through repeated asexual budding of new zooids. These harmless tentacled animals feed on minute organisms and organic material that they extract from the water.

In addition to bryozoans, tidewater boaters may also see freshwater sponges, flatworms, nematodes, leeches, oligochaete worms, and several other aquatic/wetland animals. These may be rare or abundant, but many are small, secretive, or seldom noticed except by specialists. In freshwater sections of the river in Haddam, small oligochaete worms are by far the most abundant (but inconspicuous) animal living on the river bottom.

Us

It would be a mistake not to mention humans as a significant part of the Connecticut River ecosystem. In fact, we are no doubt the most ecologically influential member of the river fauna. Our presence is greatest in the warmer months when hundreds of boaters navigate the river from sunrise to sunset (and even after dark). Our impact, however, is year-round. For example, reduced water quality stresses aquatic animals and reduces their food resources. Flood control structures alter stream flow and affect vegetation patterns and animal life histories. And oil barge traffic disrupts the rest and feeding activity of wintering waterfowl and bald eagles.

But our relationship with the river certainly isn't all negative. Because of our compassion for other forms of life, our imagination, and our sense of responsibility, we nurture and protect the river system not only as an invaluable natural resource, but also as a source of beauty, learning, and fun.

Tidewaters of the Connecticut River

Part II
The Guidebook

Site descriptions
by Thomas Maloney

Historical Notes and site descriptions
of Chester Creek and Hamburg Cove
by Carol Hardin Kimball

Introduction to Part II

Boating in the Tidewaters Region

THE TIDEWATERS of the Connecticut River have always been important to boating. Whether for trade or shipbuilding, the lower river towns have had strong ties to the Connecticut as a transportation corridor. During the 20th century, however, the river was so polluted that many towns turned their backs to it. Highways like new Route 9 and Interstate 91 were built between the river and the cities of Middletown and Hartford. Attitudes and water quality changed dramatically as a result of the federal Clean Water Act and a state commitment to clean up and restore our rivers. The Connecticut has now become a mecca for recreational boaters, anglers, naturalists, and explorers.

The following chapters will help you enjoy the premier natural areas of the Tidewaters region—its hidden coves and marshes. Each tour provides information on where to launch your boat, how far you need to travel to reach your destination, and what you'll see when you get there. We have added historical notes of interest to provide the cultural context for the natural attractions. Before you embark on your personal discovery of the Tidewaters region, we have a few overall observations and tips intended to make your experience safer and more enjoyable.

You'll find all kinds of recreational boating on the lower Connecticut. You'll see speedboats and large inboard craft, but those aren't the boats for exploring coves. The best-suited boats are canoes, kayaks, or a dinghy powered by a motor that probably is only a little stronger than the food processor in your kitchen. Not only will you avoid damage to your prop from snags and rocks, but you'll be able to get into more of the interesting small channels. You'll also be able to concentrate on the rich sounds of the many birds and insects or silence, depending on the season.

Boating on the Connecticut River is a simple, enjoyable way to spend a day. However, the river is not always a safe place to boat. Inexperienced boaters should find someone more experienced to go with, or take a boating safety or paddling class. Start with trips in protected coves and creeks before tackling the main stem. Experienced boaters should take basic precautions to avoid turning a dreamy day on the river into a nightmare. The authors of this guide have spent hundreds (even thousands!) of hours on the river. We offer the following to insure your safety on the water.

Being prepared: Spring freshets

Boating on the river can have its pitfalls, and you need to be prepared for the conditions you may encounter. During warm days in late March and early April, boaters will probably be drawn to the river, eager to begin another season of boating. However, the Connecticut River in spring can challenge even the most experienced boaters.

As the snowpack melts in the upper watershed of Vermont and New Hampshire, snowmelt water keeps the Tidewaters surprisingly colder than local streams. In fact, the river can stay cold remarkably late into spring. Wetsuits are advisable for paddlers during these times, since hypothermia could set in quickly (a matter of minutes!) if one were to capsize in these cold waters. Obviously, vast volumes of meltwater and April showers contribute to high spring river flow, as well. Life jackets or personal flotation devices are always a necessity and a must during the spring. Be sure to let someone know where you are going and when you plan to be back. That information could be life-saving if you run into trouble.

High spring flows are referred to as freshets. During a strong freshet, the river can show no evidence of a tide at all because there is just too much downstream flow—as much as four times the usual flows. These strong flows often create unexpected currents, eddies, and upwellings. Be particularly cautious of the currents and stay close to shore. The downstream sides of bridge piers often have strong eddies that have been known to flip small boats. It is best to stay close to shore and keep an eye out for snags and floating logs.

Summer on the river

Although the river provides a haven from the summer swelter, there are a number of simple common-sense considerations that will help to ensure a fun trip. First off, know the tides and try to paddle with them if possible. What could be better than having the earth, sun, and moon on your side when relaxing on the river! Many local shops carry tide charts, which give the time of high and low tide at Old Saybrook, and you will find time variations in this guide for each of the cove locations.

Similarly, watch the weather. The prevailing summer winds —the "sou'westers"— can create a sizable chop and difficult paddling. The site accounts that follow will highlight areas where the fetch (the expanse of water over which winds can generate waves) can be particularly troublesome to paddlers. Be aware that these winds can be light early and freshen throughout the day. Remember, too, it's always good to have an eye on the sky for thunderstorms. Lightning is a wonderful spectacle, but can be dangerous on the water. If you see a fast-moving storm, get to shore immediately and enjoy the show from there. Do not try to race back to the put-in.

Other common sense includes bringing drinking water, something to eat, sunscreen and insect repellent. Paddlers should yield the right-of-way to powerboats; powerboats should take care not to throw a wake that might swamp a paddler. Basically, every boater should be aware of other boaters on the water. Remember, even though you might know the rules and courtesy, others may not. Popular weekends, such as Labor Day and Memorial Day, can have an overwhelming number of boaters on the river. For paddlers this often means a day of coping with incessant boat wakes. If you're close to shore, these can rebound off of cliffs and armored banks and hit you unexpectedly.

The Fall

Perhaps the best time of year to boat on the river is late summer and early fall. The persistent and less charming of the lower river's denizens—the no-see-ums, deerflies, greenheads, and mosquitoes—have died back some, and the weather can have that particular crispness in the air that reinvigorates life in New England. Later in the fall, as the leaves start to change, pay attention to the hunting seasons. During hunting season, wear bright colors and boat during the middle part of the day. State law requires life jackets during the colder months.

Winter

In the winter, the ferries have shut down, and recreational boating is severely limited. Winter boating has its own rewards, but requires a special breed. Ice flows can occur even if the river is open. Also, the coves will freeze first, since the river's flow tends to keep it open longer. If you do decide to try the river in winter, wetsuits and life jackets are a must! Joining the "frostbiters" who sail on the river at Essex is only for the truly hardy.

Again, be sure someone knows where you are going and when you are coming back.

One more thing. With increasing use, these coves and marshes must be treated with respect. A few simple guidelines will help to insure the proper stewardship of these sites: camp only in designated sites, carry out your trash, don't create new fire rings, and obey speed limits. Each of us that enjoy the river can take small steps to minimize our impact. Through your stewardship, these habitats will continue to be internationally known and appreciated.

At any time of year, take time to notice the river, and it will offer something in return: a school of hickory shad chasing bunker literally out of the water in Lord Cove, the stoic patience of a great egret stalking minnows in Selden Creek, and the magentas, lilacs, and scarlets of a sunset at Griswold Point. The Tidewaters region has something for everyone, and the following chapters offer a glimpse into some of the best spots to visit.

Chapter 7

SALMON COVE, EAST HADDAM

SALMON COVE can be thought of as the Tidewaters region in miniature. Located at the mouth of the beautiful Salmon and Moodus rivers, Salmon Cove is a great place to boat and explore. The Salmon River watershed hosts a significant run of migratory fish and is an important stream in the effort to restore Atlantic salmon.

A natural richness

Salmon Cove is known for its beautiful freshwater tidal marshes, forested uplands, and richness of life. It is hard to miss the great and prominent stand of pickerelweed in the middle of the lower cove. Eagles roost here in the winter, ospreys are common in the warmer months, and hundreds of ducks rely on the cove for resting and feeding. Anglers tempt bass and pike with old-fashioned bait and highly engineered lures. Boaters often speak of the cove's incredible beauty—the light of a fall evening as it fades from gold to foliage-matching russet; the vibrancy of a crisp spring morning, with recently arrived songbirds declaring their territories; and the runs of fish pressing upstream. These experiences compel you to return to Salmon Cove time and time again.

Setting out

The Salmon River boat launch is maintained by the Connecticut Department of Environmental Protection (DEP) and can be a bustling place on warm weekends. For the naturalist and explorer, the floodplain forest around the boat launch area has a great deal to offer—even before setting out. In summer, listen for the languid song of the warbling vireo and look for the seemingly misnamed red-bellied woodpecker (the red on the belly isn't very noticeable). There are also stands of skunk cabbage here and there in the forest. This plant is actually capable of generating heat through metabolic processes, allowing it to flower earlier than others and gain a competitive advantage. Skunk cabbage is pollinated by flies attracted to the odor. Canoers and kayakers will want to put in to the right of the actual boat launch and hug the shore into the cove. During periods of high flow, you will definitely feel the current as you paddle upstream. Most of Salmon Cove is fairly exposed, so check the wind direction and strength before setting out. When the winds are out of the west or northwest, paddle directly across the mouth of the cove to the lee afforded by the far shore. Small side creeks can offer a haven on particularly windy days. They're also great to explore, particularly at a leisurely pace. Watch for schools of banded killifish jumping from the shallow water as your canoe approaches. These fish provide breakfast, lunch, and dinner to the largemouth bass and pike that, in turn, attract anglers to Salmon Cove.

The Connecticut DEP owns a significant portion of the land around the cove. Much of the west bank is an undeveloped buffer, for the former Connecticut Yankee nuclear power plant (now in the process of being decommissioned).

Side creeks and floodplains

The side creeks and floodplains of Salmon Cove support a plant community similar to those of the other freshwater tidal areas of the lower river. Unfortunately, invasive plants like purple loosestrife and *Phragmites* are becoming more and more dominant in some of these side marshes. The wild rice and cattails in the marshes around Cone's Point can be filled with birds during migration. In the summer months, yellow warblers and red-winged blackbirds nest here. The cove contains an exemplary floodplain habitat, although floodplain communities have been reduced by development and agricultural conversions up and down the river. Silver maples, cottonwoods, green ash, and sycamores dominate here.

Bald eagles

Salmon Cove is recognized for its importance to wintering bald eagles. As lakes and rivers in northern New England freeze up, bald eagles move south. The tidewaters now support as many as 60 eagles during a typical winter. The Salmon Cove boat launch can be a good spot to see these magnificent birds in the winter.

Scirpus Maritimus –*Freshwater tidal marshes* Art courtesy of Judy Preston

Moodus River

As you proceed up Salmon Cove, you might want to paddle into the mouth of the Moodus River. The tumble of vegetation and snags is accompanied by plenty of birdsong in the early summer. Listen for the simple phrases and mews of gray catbirds and the monotonous *Here I am! I'm here!* whistles of red-eyed vireos. Look out for brilliant cardinal flowers and sweetflag and blueflag iris. Red-shouldered hawks can be seen in this area, too. The so-called "Moodus noises" have generated a host of myths and legends about the area. These rumblings are a result of seismic activity and stress points in the bedrock that result in hundreds of tiny earthquakes.

Up the Salmon River: Spotties

You can boat as far up the Salmon River as the Leesville dam. It's interesting to see how the river's features contrast with the cove's. Look for spotted sandpipers. This is one of the few sandpiper species that nest in the lower river region. Spotties (as birders call them) are interesting because of their breeding ecology. They exhibit polyandry, a system in which each female may breed with multiple males, and the males incubate and tend the eggs. This strategy is employed by less than 1 percent of all bird species. As spotties flush, they'll often let out an alarm call, *peet sweet*, then fly low over the river with stiffly bowed wings.

Farther up the river you will pass resorts with vacationers enjoying the river. After Route 151, it's a short distance up to the Leesville dam. The notable thing about the dam is the fishway—one of the oldest in Connecticut. The fishway is owned and operated by the Connecticut DEP and allows thousands of fish access to upstream habitats. These migratory fish provide vital links in the food chain of the river.

Since Salmon Cove is so extensive, always be aware of the winds and pay attention if they're at your back as you head up the cove. Sometimes what seems to be a leisurely paddle can turn into a real workout on the trip back to the boat launch.

Historical Notes

Venture Smith: A free man of strength and integrity

Nestled between the high rock ledges of Haddam Neck—separating the Salmon River from the Connecticut—rests the stone foundation of a former slave's home. (This site is on posted Connecticut Yankee power plant land.) At age six, Venture Smith (circa 1708–1805) watched as his father, the king of West Guinea's Dudankarra tribe, was tortured to death. Soon afterward, the boy was sold to a Rhode Island ship's officer. At age 49, after serving three New England masters, Venture was able to purchase his freedom, as well as the freedom of his wife and children— one at a time. Venture and his family owned and farmed one hundred acres on Haddam Neck. He constructed three dwellings and owned a small fleet of canoes and sailing vessels. He was renowned for his strength and his integrity. Venture Smith and his wife Meg are buried in the East Haddam Congregational Church cemetery.

The Trumbull

The 700-ton ship *Trumbull*, one of thirteen large frigates commissioned by Congress, was built in Middletown in 1777. However, her ten-and-a-half-foot draft kept her from being able to pass over the nine-foot-deep Saybrook Bar. And so she was stripped of her spars and hidden in the Salmon River. Three years later, on August 11, 1779, supported by a "necklace" of air-filled barrels that reduced her draft, the *Trumbull* passed over the bar. Her service was brief, as she was forced to surrender to two British men-of-war the following summer after a bloody three-hour battle.

Captain Olmstead: Privateer

In response to the British blockade of commercial shipping during the War of 1812, American ships were commissioned as privateers. One of the most daring privateer captains was East Haddam's Gideon Olmstead. He was twice captured by the British, but to no avail. He died in 1845 at the age of 97.

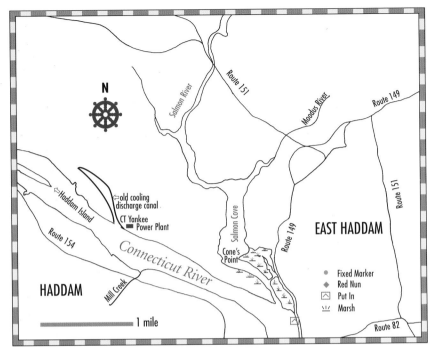

SALMON COVE ACCESS TABLE

Access Point
  Route 9, exit 7, east on Route 82 over East Haddam bridge. Left just past Goodspeed Opera House on Route 149 north, 1.1 miles turn left.

Guidelines
  State boat launch at the junction of Connecticut and Salmon rivers; parking for over 40 cars with trailers.

Off the Ramp Directions
  Paddle right along shore, right into Salmon River.

Water/Marsh Type
  Freshwater tidal marsh

Distance from Lynde Point Lighthouse
  16.6 miles

Tidal Range
  Mean 2.9 feet, highest tidal range 3.5 feet

Nearest Store
  Cheeseboard Deli, Routes 154 and 82, Tylerville (Haddam)

Notes
  Salmon Cove is an open body of water that can pose challenges to the paddler during high winds. It's also a very popular fishing and boating spot, so be alert for other boats. Paddlers should not use the ramp during busy days, since they can launch small boats off the side, but power-boaters using trailers must use the ramp.

on

Preston 96

Eastern Elliptic   Elliptio complanata

Chapter 8

CHAPMAN POND AND CREEK, EAST HADDAM

FOR CONSERVATIONISTS, Chapman Pond is particularly notable for the large concentrations of waterfowl that feed there during the late fall and winter. If you paddle into Chapman Pond on an October day, you'll see several species of ducks, including wood ducks and blue-winged and green-winged teal. Less noticeable but still abundant at that time are sora rails that stop off during migration to fuel up on the wild rice growing in Chapman and the river's other freshwater tidal marshes. Later in the year, hundreds of black ducks and mallards call Chapman Pond home for the winter.

It's a comfort when boating in the pond and along Chapman Creek to know that all but a few parcels of the land bordering the cove are owned by private or state conservation organizations. The Connecticut DEP, The Nature Conservancy, and the East Haddam Land Trust are the landlords here. They continue to work together to protect this Connecticut River treasure.

Setting Out

The boat launch by the East Haddam airport affords the closest point of entry on the same side of the river. Beware of boat wakes and occasional strong wind, as you set out downstream. The tides here range about two and a half feet, but they don't pose too much of a challenge to a paddler. It's easy to observe ospreys, three gull species, double-crested cormorants, and an occasional bald eagle (in winter) as you paddle to the creek entrance. Stay left inside of Rich Island and, between the island and the shore, look out for belted kingfishers and green herons. Toward the southern end of Rich Island look for the entrance to Chapman Pond on the left.

The Great Ditch

You'll notice a creek that leads you east toward the pond. Interestingly, this creek is not a creek: it's a man-made canal. A dispute a century or so ago between commercial shad fishermen and a landowner caused the landowner to block passage of the shad netters' boats down Chapman Creek. So they dug "the Great Ditch." The ditch has naturally widened over the years. The shores of the ditch have grown in beautifully with characteristic wetland and floodplain plants such as silver maple, green ash, cottonwood, red-osier dogwood, and buttonbush. Unfortunately, you will notice that these native species are being overgrown by Oriental bittersweet, a non-native invasive vine.

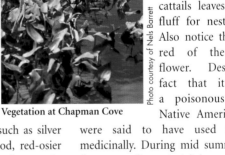

Vegetation at Chapman Cove

Photo courtesy of Nels Barrett

Ospreys

References to Chapman Meadow and its south-flowing creek begin in the 1700s. The pond is a result of a lot of things, including rising sea level. As you enter the pond from the Great Ditch, keep your head up. Waterfowl and wading birds often flush at the first sign of boaters entering the pond. In the late summer, keep an eye out for herons and egrets; later in the year

bald eagles are a possibility. At any time during the warmer months (and even into early November), ospreys frequent Chapman Pond. It's no accident that fish-eating ospreys return to the river at just about the same time as large schools of migratory fishes. Chapman Pond is a very important spawning site for alewives, which serve a vital role in the food chains of Chapman Pond, the lower river, and Long Island Sound as well.

Pickerelweed and other plants

You might want to circumnavigate the pond before heading south along Chapman Creek. If you do, take time to note the structure of the plant community. Low perennial emergents like pickerelweed, with its large arrow-shaped leaves and spike of blue flowers, provide cover to frogs, fish, and turtles. Pickerelweed gives way to cattails and wild rice, which provide food and cover to a number of species. Muskrats use cattail as their primary food and for building their lodges. Many birds use cattails leaves and seed fluff for nest building. Also notice the brilliant red of the cardinal flower. Despite the fact that it contains a poisonous alkaloid, Native American tribes were said to have used the plant medicinally. During mid summer, watch for rose mallow, virgin's bower, blue flag, and yellow iris.

Going south

Heading south along Chapman Creek, you'll find a new discovery around each bend. Notice the invasive *Phragmites* on the floodplain to the west. The Nature Conservancy and the Connecticut DEP are intensively controlling this stand through removal efforts. As you approach the mouth of Chapman Creek at the Connecticut River, beware of the dead trees and limbs. Paddlers can get through, but powerboaters should be cautious.

Going slowly will allow you to notice the stand of wild rice and large green ash trees, many covered by huge poison ivy vines, at the creek's mouth. During migration periods, these trees can be alive with birds.

From this point you can either return up the Connecticut or retrace your way up into the pond. If you go the creek-to-pond route, you stand a better chance of seeing wildlife.

Historical Notes

The Goodspeed legacy

William H. Goodspeed was East Haddam's most famous 19th-century entrepreneur. He owned the ferry where the 1913 swing bridge now sits, constructed ships at Goodspeed's Landing below, and won a contract to build an experimental steam-powered gunboat, the *Kanawa*, for the U.S. Navy during the Civil War. After building the Gelston House to encourage steamboat tourists to stay a while in East Haddam, he opened the six-story Goodspeed Opera House in 1877— a multi-use structure that included stores and commercial operations. Goodspeed died in 1882.

The Chapman of Chapman Pond

In 1642, Robert Chapman of Saybrook became the first European to acquire land south of Hartford from a Native American. Accounts differ as to whether he purchased the land from a Mohegan named Chapeto or was given it by Wequash, a Nehantic ally of Uncas and the English in their struggles against the Pequots. In the 17th century Chapman Meadow was a broad floodplain, without a pond, draining the Seven Sister Hills, and stretching from below the Goodspeed Opera House south to Gillette Castle's promontory. Chapman Pond was probably created by an early-18th-century flood, since that is when the name first appeared. Today, the Gelston House stands where Robert's son, Captain John Chapman, built his home in 1673 overlooking the floodplain.

Haying and the Great Flood of 1936

By the 19th century, Chapman Pond was known for its high-quality marsh hay (used as winter feed and bedding for cattle), even though the river and pond waters are almost entirely fresh. On average, it took three tons of hay to keep an animal throughout the winter. There are still people who remember the community hay harvests, using cradle scythes to cut the hay, piling the bales high onto carts, and then hauling the carts by oxen teams across a stone culvert at the Great Ditch. The Great Flood of 1936 brought the haying era to an abrupt end, depositing tons of silt and debris over the meadows, washing out the culvert, and creating a large island which, to this day, has no name.

Tobacco and oyster-shell buttons

In the late 1800s, Maltby Gelston built a house at the base of a hill on the eastern edge of Chapman Pond, directly across from the Great Ditch. He grew tobacco and received a patent for a cigar-rolling process he devised. A later owner of the property made oyster-shell buttons. Although the house was destroyed by fire in 1971, buttons still turn up now and then on the grounds.

Enter Mr. Gillette

William H. Gillette (1850–1937) was most renowned for his role as Sherlock Holmes (he gave over 1,300 performances). He also wrote 20 plays and built a model steam engine for Pratt & Whitney. Son of U.S. Senator Francis Gillette, a Hartford abolitionist and descendant of Thomas Hooker, Gillette was encouraged to enter the "sinful" acting profession by Mark Twain. From 1914 to 1919, he built his 24-room, cobbled-stone castle, inspired by a Norman fortress, on the highest of the Seven Sisters, above the Hadlyme ferry. Gillette ferried his numerous guests to and from New York on his 140-foot houseboat, the *Aunt Polly*. Many also enjoyed the 3-mile journey on his miniature railroad. The remains of his dock pilings are still visible at low tide north of the ferry landing.

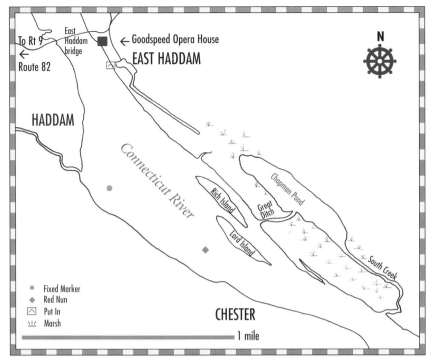

Chapman Pond Access Table

Access Point
Route 9, exit 7, east on Route 82 over East Haddam bridge.
Past Goodspeed Opera House, turn right down hill after Gelston House
toward airport. Right turn into access lane just before airport.

Guidelines
Town of East Haddam property, car-top only. Unpaved limited parking.
Do not use the airport launch (the larger launch just past town launch) it is for
float planes and is private property.

Off the Ramp Directions
Paddle down the river along shore for approximately 1 mile; turn left into the
Great Ditch, which flows into Chapman Pond.

Water/Marsh type
Freshwater tidal marsh

Distance from Lynde Point Lighthouse
14 miles

Tidal Range
Mean 2.9 feet / highest tidal range 3.5 feet

Nearest Store
Cheeseboard Deli, Routes 154 and 82, Tylerville (Haddam).

Notes
Chapman Pond and Creek are easy paddling. However, winds and boat wakes
on the open water of the Connecticut can be challenging. Stay alert for other
boats and use the lees afforded by Rich and Lord islands. Round-trip distance is
about 3 miles. High tide is 1 hour, 31 minutes after tide table listing
for Old Saybrook Jetty.

Chapter 9

CHESTER CREEK AND COVE, CHESTER

CHESTER CREEK has been called "a virtual water garden," and its abundant botanical life and wildlife have been well documented. The Nature Conservancy's 1994 survey of submerged aquatic vegetation mapped the locations of major beds and discovered 13 species, mainly in the broad marsh expanses west of Route 154. In 1996, a vegetative survey commissioned by the Chester Land Trust identified 103 species: 7 trees, 22 shrubs, 51 non-woody plants, 3 ferns, 5 vines, and 15 rushes, grasses, and sedges. A 1997 inventory of fauna, also commissioned by the land trust, turned up a similar level of diversity, and in 1996 one observer listed 162 species of birds.

The creek's calm waters and rich plant life create superb habitat for fish. Consequently, reptilian and avian fish predators abound—snapping turtles and ospreys in summer, bald eagles in winter. Although the dams above today's Chester Village limit the ability of anadromous fish to spawn in upstream waters of Pattaconk and Great brooks, historically Chester Creek has served as a natural hatchery for 25 species, including sea lamprey, alewife, blueback herring, sea-run brown trout, smelt, and white perch. Both largemouth and smallmouth bass winter in the creek, and you might spot their nests in mid-June—look for their hollowed-out, 2 foot-wide depressions in the channel. Perch also congregate in the area.

Setting Out

The best place to put in is at the Carini Preserve. The 6-acre preserve, which officially opened in September 2000, lies at the confluence of Great and Pattaconk brooks. The two brooks merge to become Chester Creek. The Chester Land Trust worked for five years to assemble the preserve, acquiring and combining several small parcels. The acreage was choked with Japanese knotweed and other invasive plants, but volunteers gradually cleared the site, replanting with native wetland flora such as cardinal flower, great lobelia, buttonbush, and umbrella sedge. A picnic table provides a welcome touch to this wetland restoration in progress.

Because the upper reaches of Chester Creek are shallow, the optimal time to arrive or depart from the Carini Preserve is on a rising half tide. High tide on the river (at the entrance to Chester Creek) follows the high at the Old Saybrook Jetty by 1 hour, 50 minutes, and takes another 20 to reach the Carini Preserve. So, high tide at Carini is approximately 2 hours, 10 minutes after Old Saybrook.

The Pattaconk River

Until the early 19th century, the entire waterway was called the Pattaconk River. At that time, it cut a fairly deep channel all the way from the mouth of the Connecticut River up to the very center of Chester, then called the "Head of the Cove." Today, "the cove" refers to the wide marshy area west of the Connecticut Valley Railroad trestle through which flows Chester Creek, the now-diminished Pattaconk River. Altogether, the area encompasses roughly 125 acres of freshwater tidal marsh, 50 acres of which are currently owned by the Chester Land Trust.

The end of an era

The completion in 1816 of the Middlesex Turnpike's causeway—followed by the construction of the Valley Railroad's trestle

in 1871—guaranteed the demise of shipbuilding at the "Head of the Cove" in Chester Center. The relatively deep navigation channel began to silt in, and further maritime development west of the Turnpike (today's Route 154) was blocked. Chester Creek's isolation was assured, allowing it to continue, undisturbed, as an exceptional example of a freshwater tidal wetland.

Along Chester Creek

Before setting off downstream from the Carini Preserve, pause a moment and imagine that the year is 1800, when the creek was deeper. A schooner moves slowly upstream, on a rising tide, in the lee of Laurel Hill's steep wooded slope. She's headed to one of Chester Center's 18th-century wharves to unload cargo from the West Indies, and perhaps to purchase a new anchor at Able Snow's Anchor Foundry on the Pattaconk. The building on this site once housed the National Theatre for the Deaf and is now home to the Chester Historical Society.

While paddling the initial stretch of shallow creek below the put-in, notice the streambanks lined to the water by thickets of speckled alder, silky dogwood, and other vegetation typical of a red maple swamp. The creek then makes an "S" north and then east, paralleling Route 148. However, the thick protective border of upland woods screens out the cars. Soon the paddler's vista broadens as the marsh widens and Chester Creek's rich diversity of plant and animal life becomes more apparent. Depending on the season, large stands of pickerelweed, arrowarum, or wild rice dominate, interspersed with bright patches of blue flag, yellow golden club, or deep purple New York ironweed. You might spot a muskrat scuttling off through the reeds, or a great blue heron. At low tide, green herons, and even an occasional goldfinch, feed on the mudflats.

From the Causeway to the Connecticut

Once you've reached the causeway's bridge, the combination of tide, time, and your inclination will determine whether to return upstream to the Carini Preserve or to continue on to the mainstream river—about 3/4 mile farther east. If you decide to continue on, after paddling under "Denison's Bridge," you will take another leisurely "Swing before passing under the railroad trestle. In summer, you're likely to see (and you're certain to hear) the Essex Steam Train en route north to Haddam or returning south to Essex.

Just past the railroad trestle, WaterHouse Creek joins Chester Creek from the north. At that juncture, there's a fine view north to Gillette Castle. Within a few yards the yacht basins and

Gillette Castle in winter.

Photo courtesy of © Robert Benson

marinas gain the upper hand, monopolizing both banks on out to the river. This stretch can be crowded on summer weekends!

From Chester Creek's entrance on the river, it's about a 20-minute paddle north to the Chester- Hadlyme Ferry. Or, it's fun to simply paddle around near the entrance enjoying the panoramic view upriver, across to Selden Island and south to Deep River.

Whether approached from east or west, a visit to Chester Creek's variety of habitats is certainly worthwhile.

Historical Notes

Pattaquonunk to Pattaconk
Chester's Native Americans, the Wanguks, centered their territory at "Pattaquonunk," their hilltop fort above today's Chester Ferry Landing. By 1740, Pattaquonunk (which means "round or wigwam-shaped hill") had evolved to "Pattaconk," the name of Saybrook Colony's northern quarter, as well as its major brook. Today's marshes were known as the Pattaconk River Valley, a broad open expanse with a navigable channel as far inland as Chester's village center, then called the "Head of the Cove."

Shipbuilding and commerce
In the 18th century and early 19th century, trading vessels bound for the West Indies or the Maritimes docked at the Stevens & Colt or the Leet & Buck wharves in the "Head of the Cove." Primary early exports were cedar shingles (from the nearby extensive cedar swamp) and barrel staves made from local hickory. Mercantile house owners also constructed ships: Pardon Stevens and Samuel Colt's yard fronted their headquarters at Main and Maple (Bonfanti's Real Estate). On the north side of the Pattaconk's arched bridge sat the Old Building Yard. There, in 1795,

Gideon Leet and William Buck constructed the 65-foot, 97-ton, two-masted brig *Matilda*, which French privateers seized off Guadeloupe in the West Indies in 1797. Despite the loss, by 1809 Leet and Buck were able to expand their original merchant house, constructing the granite-columned stone building (Cummings & Good Graphic Design) there today.

Bani Denison
Bani Denison monopolized economic activity at the busy juncture of the Middlesex Turnpike/Route 154 and Ferry Road/Route 148. His merchant house, on the northeast corner above his shipbuilding yard on the creek's bank, served as tavern, tollhouse, stagecoach stop, store, and post office. Later, the building was moved back from the water and restored; today, it is One Ferry Road. Although the wily Irishman picked up some shipbuilding business from the "Head of the Cove" after 1816, Chester shipbuilding began to decline with the increasing demand for larger vessels. From 1830 on, the balance shifted in favor of Bani's descendants, Thomas and Eli Denison's yard on Deep River's waterfront.

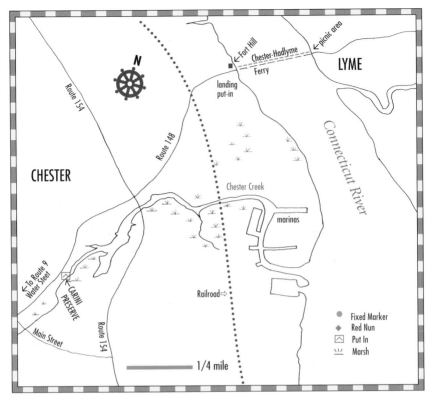

Chester Cove and Creek Access Table

Access Point
Route 9, exit 6, east on Route 148 (Water Street) to four-way stop in Chester Village Center. Carini Preserve is 1/10th mile farther on right adjacent to Great Brook.

Guidelines
Car-top only. Owned by Chester Land Trust. Small boat drop-off only, parking in town lot, same side. (Access from mouth of creek at Chester or Hays Haven Marinas $10 to launch plus $10 to park.)

Off the Ramp Directions
Paddle downstream to mouth of creek.

Water/Marsh Type
Freshwater tidal marsh

Distance from Lynde Point Lighthouse
11.5 miles

Tidal Range
Mean 2.7 feet / highest tidal range 3.2 feet

Nearest Store
The Wheatmarket, behind 4 Water Street (Route 148), plus several others close by in Chester Village Center.

Notes
Chester Creek's calm, protected waters offer ideal canoeing and kayaking. From the north, it's a 20-minute paddle from the Chester-Hadlyme Ferry south hugging the western shore.

½ x

ONE INCH

PRESTON 95

Chapter 10

WHALEBONE COVE, LYME

REACHING WHALEBONE COVE is very easy. It's just a few hundred yards from the Gillette Castle State Park boat launch to the cove's entrance. The access, at the far end of the parking lot, is car-top only. Be aware of the crossing Chester-Hadlyme Ferry (it crosses the river in just four minutes.) Always yield the right-of-way to the ferry. It is recommended to cross the ferry lane just after it has pulled away into the middle of the river or when it is docked on the Chester side.

The ferry, incidentally, is the second oldest continuously operating ferry in the United States and has been carrying people from Hadlyme to Chester and back since 1769.

Whalebone Creek: Granite and hemlocks

The mouth of Whalebone Creek is on the east side of the river just downstream from the boat launch at the high bedrock outcrop. The Connecticut is quite busy here, although southwest winds in the summer can make the short paddle a bit more daunting. The mouth of Whalebone Creek is a great place to examine the rock of the lower Connecticut. This large cliff of granitic schist, a remnant of Avalonia from a continental collision millions of years ago, has clearly resisted the erosive effects of the river. Like many bedrock outcrops in the Tidewaters, this area is dominated by hemlocks. You'll notice, however, that the hemlocks are not very healthy. That's because of the hemlock woolly adelgid, an invasive non-native insect that is destroying most of the hemlocks in the lower Connecticut River valley.

Vireos and warblers

Upon entering Whalebone Cove, you'll immediately forget the fetch and bustle of the river. As you make your way toward the open expanse of the cove in spring and summer, you'll be serenaded by scores of birds. Listen specifically for two contrasting song styles: the short jumble of a white-eyed vireo and the dry steady chipping of the worm-eating warbler. These birds differ in habitats as well. The vireo prefers the tangle of the floodplain growth (including lots of wild grapes) south of the channel, while the warbler remains in the dry wooded slope to the north.

Floodplain vegetation and herons and egrets

Dogwoods, speckled alder, and buttonbush dominate the shrubs along the shore. You'll also notice sycamores and ashes, which provide roosting sites for great blue herons and snowy egrets. It's not uncommon to flush

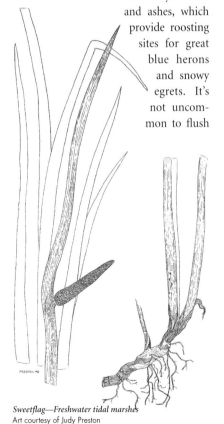

Sweetflag—Freshwater tidal marshes
Art courtesy of Judy Preston

these birds while traveling along Whalebone Creek. Listen for the prehistoric-sounding croak of a startled great blue heron. Check the trees for ospreys, too. They often perch there to devour their catch of the day, perhaps a bass, or in the spring, American shad. Whalebone Creek hosts a run of spawning anadromous fishes. A spring trip might coincide with migratory runs of alewife and sea lamprey. Look for schools of fish heading to the farthest reaches of the cove, where Roaring Brook, the main inflowing stream, enters the cove. Native chain pickerel occur here with the non-native residents, bluegills and largemouth bass, for a short period while spawning.

Wild rice

Farther along, the creek and cove begin to open up. It quickly becomes apparent why this is considered one of the special freshwater coves of the lower river. Notice the large stands of wild rice, for which Whalebone Cove is best known. This annual grass grows up to 15 feet tall. In the late summer it is ripe with the prized grain. Then and later into the fall, birds abound in Whalebone Cove. Red-winged blackbirds, black ducks, wood ducks, and soras descend on Whalebone to feast on the grain and prepare for the migration ahead. Other dominant wetland plants in the marsh are cattails and bulrushes. Also notice the large patches of submerged aquatic vegetation underwater. These plants provide cover for fish and food for waterfowl.

Side channels

As you continue, you'll notice several side channels that merit exploration. Paddling silently during high tide is the best way to explore these creeks. You're likely to encounter painted and snapping turtles along the way. A quiet splash from a log or rock is likely to have been a basking painted turtle. Usually, these creeks narrow progressively until they are choked out by vegetation. Even so, they provide terrific opportunities to observe nature. If you're silent enough, you'll have an excellent opportunity to observe Whalebone's wildlife, including swamp sparrows, marsh

Phragmites and autumn vegetation

wrens (in the early summer the males will entertain you with their territorial flight song), muskrats, river otters, and mink. After exploring the side channels, it's fun to go right to the head of the cove where Roaring Brook enters. In recent years, a beaver has taken up residence here and has built a dam that occasionally gets back-flooded at high tide. This is a good spot to watch sunfish build or aggressively defend their nests. The red maples and speckled alders hang over the creek and provide hunting perches for belted kingfishers (their loud rattling call can be startling in the afternoon's silence). As you head back out of the creek, watch for the large floating leaves and yellow blossoms of spatterdock. This floating aquatic plant is in the water lily family and provides cover to fish, turtles, and other aquatic animals. Pickerelweed is also common here and is distinguished by its dense blue-purple flower spike. Other plants you might find include arrow-arum, arrowhead, water purslane, and rushes (soft rush and bulrush). Certainly, one of the most recognizable plants in Whalebone Cove is the blue flag iris.

Historical Notes

The Counting House

The 18th-century Counting House, with its balcony wrapped around a huge ash, sits hard by the ferry slip. Over the centuries, it served a number of purposes: as a collection point for ferry tolls, a shipyard commissary, and finally, a general store last operated by Gershom Simpson in the 1920s.

Comstock Shipyard

Isaac Spencer built the large, handsome Federal house (circa 1780) just south of the Counting House. Together with his sons, Austin and William, he established the shipyard there that was taken over by Henry T. Comstock about 1820. On the bank just above the ferry landing, the Comstocks constructed ships for the brownstone trade until 1888, including two of the largest three-masted schooners built on the river. Today's canoe launch might have been their skidway.

The Hamilton Sisters

Dr. Alice Hamilton, the first female professor at Harvard Medical School, summered with her sisters in the Spencer House. Dr. Hamilton retired there in 1945 and was often visited by her equally distinguished sister, Edith Hamilton, president of Bryn Mawr College and author of *The Greek Way* and other books on mythology. Dr. Hamilton was posthumously honored in 1995 by the issuance of a 55-cent stamp recognizing her pioneering research in occupational diseases. The Hamilton sisters, Gershom Simpson, and Austin Spencer are all buried at the nearby Cove Cemetery on Ferry Road (Route 148) overlooking Whalebone Cove.

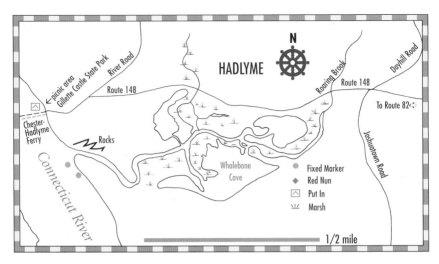

Whalebone Cove Access Table

Access Point
Adjacent to the Chester-Hadlyme Ferry landing, Route 148, 1.7 miles west of Hadlyme-Four Corners junction with Route 82.

Guidelines
Gillette Castle State Park, Connecticut DEP, Town of Lyme, car-top only, unpaved parking for 20 cars.

Off the Ramp Directions
Paddle down Connecticut River approximately 1,000 feet; take a left into Whalebone Creek, which leads you to Whalebone Cove.

Water/Marsh Type
Freshwater tidal marsh

Distance from Lynde Point Lighthouse
12.3 miles.

Tidal Range
Mean 2.8 feet / highest tidal range 3.4 feet

Nearest Store
Hadlyme General Store, 3.3 miles up Route 148

Notes
For the paddler, Whalebone is an easy trip. Cautions include maneuvering around the Chester-Hadlyme Ferry landing and the short trip along the mainstream Connecticut River. These do not pose particularly daunting challenges, however.

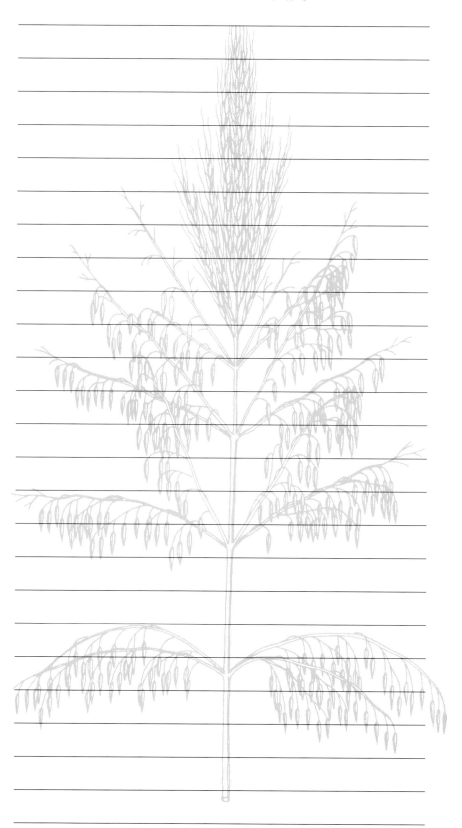

Chapter 11

HAMBURG COVE, LYME

HAMBURG COVE'S lower bay is crowded with boats on summer weekends. It's best appreciated during the week, or on weekends before Memorial Day or after Labor Day. The picturesque upper bay—about a mile up the cove—is navigable by kayak, canoe, and small boat up to the Joshuatown Bridge and a half-mile beyond during the spring. Hamburg Cove has long been prized as a safe anchorage in stormy weather and as the first major inlet where sailing ships could moor and let the Eightmile River's fresh water help rid their hulls of barnacles and algae. Described by the *Boston Transcript* in 1817 as "an earthly paradise," the cove's varied topography—former stately hemlock stands, luxuriant mountain laurel, and farmed hillsides—has long inspired artists.

Setting Out

Hamburg Cove comprises the lower portion of the Eightmile River as it flows into the Connecticut. Green Can #1 and Red Nun #2 mark the narrow entrance to the 9-foot-deep channel that leads into the

Lower Bay, the principal anchorage area, about two-thirds of a mile long. Unless you're in a canoe or kayak, it's important to remain within the channel.

Abigail's Hole
Abigail's Hole, the shallow, secluded little cove north of Green Can #5, was likely named in honor of Abigail Niles (Mrs. Comfort Tiffany), who died in 1738. Ospreys, great blue herons, black-crowned night herons, and the occasional bald eagle fish and roost in its bordering elms and hickories. Just south of Abigail's Hole on Fishing Point, you'll notice the Elijah Ely house and its grass-covered dock. Built about 1765, it's the oldest dwelling on the cove.

Flat Rock and The Narrows
Until the 1920s, Flat Rock, on the Lower Bay's east shore, supported an ice house in which locally cut blocks were stored, awaiting shipment to New York. Farther on, oaks and dead hemlocks on the high northern ledge above The Narrows provide winter perches for bald eagles. Until 1985, dense groves of eastern hemlock dominated the cove's shores. That year, Hurricane Gloria brought with it the hemlock woolly adelgid, a non-native invasive insect. The adelgid attaches itself to a hemlock's twigs, desiccating the tree by sucking out its sap. All along the river, gigantic gray hemlock skeletons bear witness to the devastation caused by the adelgid, but it has been especially dramatic in Hamburg Cove.

Falls Brook and Upper Bay
After The Narrows, Hamburg Cove widens again into the shallow Upper Bay. Ice fishing for eels is an occasional sight here in winter, and white perch draw avid anglers in March. Falls Brook, which drains a portion of Nehantic State Forest, enters the east side of the Upper Bay, flowing beneath Cove Road. A variety of freshwater plants is evident. Wild rice, buttonbush, blue flag, sneezeweed, and cardinal flower appear on the shores and along the uncommon cobble flats just above the Joshuatown Bridge. Since 1680, when a sawmill was built at the foot of Mount Archer—a half mile upriver from the Joshuatown Bridge—anadromous fish have been unable to ascend the Eightmile past the mill's 9-foot Rathbun Dam to access the calm, upstream freshwater they must have to spawn. Three centuries later, in 1997, a fishway was opened, bypassing the mill and dam. Alewives, blueback herring, sea-run brown trout, bass, suckers, eels, and sea lampreys now can travel as far up as Devil's Hopyard. A second fishway was installed in 2000 at Ed Bill's Dam on the east branch of the Eightmile. Restoring populations of anadromous fishes expands the forage base, improving the overall freshwater ecosystem and supporting otters, minks, snapping turtles, kingfishers, and ospreys, to name but a few.

The *Tansy Bitters* at Hamburg Cove

Hamburg Cove, Cove Landing

Historical Notes

Joshua's Rock

Best observed from Great Meadow, Joshua's Rock stands sentinel on the eastern shore of the Connecticut just north of Hamburg Cove. From his special stone seat on the promontory, Chief Joshua, son of Uncas, renowned last Mohegan sachem, reputedly loved observing his people as they fished in the river below.

Reed's Landing shipyard

Around 1710, William Sterling founded one of the lower river's earliest shipyards at Reed's Landing, just below the Joshuatown Bridge. There, up to 40 men took months to construct one small 40-to-50 foot vessel for the coastal trade. Each hull was hewn from white oak, the masts and booms from white pine, the whole held together with locust wood trunnels (wooden "tree nails") and caulked with tarred oakum. Once launched, the hull was floated down to Flat Rock on outer Hamburg Cove, where the mast was stepped. The ship was fully rigged out in Essex.

Historic homes

Nothing remains of the 18th-century structures supporting the Reed's Landing shipyard. However, the buildings presently below the bridge are remarkably unchanged from those depicted in George F. Bottum's large 1840 painting of Reed's Landing hanging in the Lyme Town Hall. Gambrel-roofed 29 Joshuatown Road, built in 1803 for Captain William Johnston, was used as the local Masonic Hall. In 1905, the house became the summer home of noted Lyme Art Colony painter George Breustle, and later of his son Bertram, also an artist.

The Reynolds legacy

Today's best-known Hamburg waterfront family businesses got their start when Ephraim O. Reynolds established a carriage shop in 1859. His son Hayden, transformed the upstairs of their trading post into the H. L. Reynolds Co. General Store, currently owned and operated by Ephraim's great-granddaughter, Jane Reynolds DeWolf. The carriage company would become Reynolds Garage and Marine; today it is operated by the fifth and sixth generations of the Reynolds family.

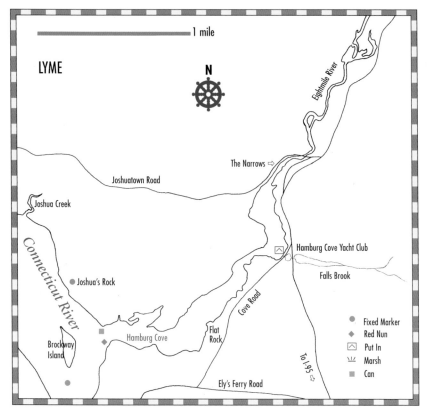

Hamburg Cove Access Table

Access Point

I-95, exit 70, north on Route 156 4.7 miles. Left after green "Hamburg" sign at Falls Brook, or 2/10 mile farther to sharp left turn on Cove Road.

Guidelines

Unmarked narrow launch site next to Hamburg Cove Yacht Club. Town of Lyme public access, car-top only, limited parking across Cove Road; no parking in the Yacht Club lot.

Off the Ramp Directions

Paddle right up the cove into lower Eightmile River above Joshuatown Road bridge. Paddle left to outer cove toward Connecticut River.

Water/Marsh Type

Brackish tidal marsh

Distance from Lynde Point Lighthouse

8 miles

Tidal Range

Mean 2.7 feet / highest tidal range 3.2 feet

Nearest Store

H. L. Reynolds Co., General Store (est. 1859) on Route 156 in Hamburg

Notes

Paddling is easy in Hamburg Cove's protected waters. Watch out for boat traffic.

ONE INCH

PRESTON 95

Chapter 12

SELDEN CREEK, LYME

FOR THE BOATER, Selden Creek offers a wonderful opportunity to leave the mainstream river and explore one of the richest freshwater tidal ecosystems in the Northeast. While Selden is a favored destination for naturalists, its plentiful fish and waterfowl attract anglers and duck hunters as well. Every season has its special features in Selden, although the winter and early spring are often prohibitively cold for boating.

Setting Out

The best boating access is at the Chester-Hadlyme Ferry landing on Route 148 in Lyme. The DEP has installed a car-top-only boat launch as part of the

Gillette Castle State Park, with plenty of parking. Beware of the ferry as you put in and head south; it's best to wait until the ferry departs for Chester and then paddle across its route after the wake has subsided. The ferry takes about four minutes to cross the river, so keep that in mind if you see it coming from the Chester side. This part of the Connecticut River is very popular for powerboating and is home to several major marinas. In addition, the breadth of the river here creates a sizable chop in strong winds. Consider these factors as you head out.

Entrance

The entrance to Selden Creek is about a mile downstream from the ferry landing.

Although this is not a long distance, inexperienced paddlers may think it's much farther than it is because of the wind, chop, and boat wakes.

About a quarter mile downstream you'll pass the mouth of Whalebone Cove on your left. As you head downriver, keep your head up for ospreys, double-crested cormorants, and gulls. (In the winter, the ferry landing is an excellent place to observe bald eagles.) There is a large private pier just over halfway to the mouth of Selden Creek. Do not try to paddle under it; stay on the outside.

As you get to the mouth of Selden Creek, you'll find that the wind and waves fade away. On the left is a small stand of wild rice. Viburnums and dogwoods dominate the shrub layer, while ashes, cottonwoods, red and silver maples, and sycamores are common trees. Where there is room, cattails, arrowhead, and arrow-arum pop up in flooded areas.

Camping
Soon you'll see the campsites along the opposite shore. Selden Creek features one of the few opportunities to camp on the lower river. Camping at Selden presents a rare opportunity to explore these habitats at dawn and dusk, when many animals are more active. You must register early for these popular campsites that are maintained by the Department of Environmental Protection out of Gillette Castle State Park (telephone number 860-526-2336.) Summer weekends are often booked solid by April 1.

The Neck becomes an island
In 1696, Joseph Selden purchased Twelve Mile Island Farm—4,000 acres including Selden Island. Back then, the island was actually a peninsula called The Neck. Later, it would be extensively quarried for granite with streaks of rose-colored quartz, used for curbing in New York City and elsewhere. In 1854, a severe late spring freshet permanently breached the north end, creating

Selden Island and depositing huge quantities of silt in the cove and creek. Today, Selden Island is there for the exploring.

Birds
The creek joins Selden Cove, an area that supported a Native American village prior to European settlement. The main creek channel turns to the hard right (or south). This is a terrific area to observe ospreys, great egrets, great blue herons, and belted kingfishers. Listen for the sapsucker-like call of the red-shouldered hawks that breed on the eastern bank of Selden Creek. In fall, Selden can be quite productive as a birding destination. Fruiting dogwoods, viburnums, and rice entice birds to descend to fuel up for their migrations south. In the early fall, you can also see large mixed flocks of warblers, tanagers, and orioles.

Selden Rock

Photo courtesy of © Robert Benson

Turtles and snakes
Watch for painted turtles sunbathing on rocks and logs. Large snapping turtles are also common in Selden. Northern water snakes are also quite common in Selden Creek and can be seen sunning or swimming with just their noses sticking up out of the water. These snakes are not venomous; they prey on frogs, small fish, and rodents.

Flowers and insects
As you head down the creek, it's difficult not to be impressed by the diversity of the plant community. Selden is a paradise for the botanist. Virgin's bower, blue flag iris, Joe-Pye weed, ironweed, and monkey flower are some of the flowers to find there. The brilliant scarlet of cardinal flower is unmistakable when in bloom. In the summer, the purple-blue spike of the pickerelweed and the yellow blossoms of the spatterdock will show up the drab flowers of rushes and sedges. Dragonflies abound and can provide the entertainment on a lazy paddle. With evocative names like pondhawk, skimmer, and clubtail, they are fascinating to watch.

Side creeks

Selden has a few side creeks that are nice diversions from your set route. About half-way down on the east side, there is a small creek that leads back to a small island in the marsh that is private property. Thankfully, 250 acres of the high land adjacent to this portion of the marsh have been conserved by the State of Connecticut in partnership with The Nature Conservancy. Farther down—in sight of the Connecticut—there are side creeks both to the east and toward Selden Island that merit exploration. Boating up the increasingly narrow side creeks can allow close observation and study of the plants and sometimes surprising views of wildlife. In the spring and early summer, look for spawning alewife and sunfish here.

Back on the Connecticut

The wind picks up as the creek widens to rejoin the Connecticut River. Just at the confluence there is a sandbar in the river where you can stretch your legs. Look for ospreys, herring gulls, black-backed gulls, and ring-billed gulls there. From this "beach," you can notice just how extensive the marsh at the south end of Selden really is. American kestrels occasionally hawk insects over this broad expanse of marsh. From this point you are left with a choice: head back up Selden Creek and continue to explore, or head up the main stem of the river around Selden Island to the ferry landing. If you stay in the creek, you'll be sheltered from the wind and wakes.

Historical Notes

Quarrying

After the Civil War, quarrying on the river boomed, primarily to pave the streets of New York and Philadelphia, but also to build breakwaters, lighthouse bases, and bridges. Irish-American entrepreneurs from Brooklyn established the Connecticut Valley Granite & Mining Company in 1890 and leased the existing quarries at Deep River, Selden Island, Brockway Landing, and Joshua's Rock, known for their unusually dense granite. On Selden Island alone, 600 mainly immigrant Irish and Italian stonecutters toiled at four quarries from May to October, sleeping and eating in company-built barracks. A narrow-gauge railroad carried the cut gneiss to schooners docked at the three wharves on the river. The company went bankrupt in 1903, and the quarries were rapidly abandoned.

Brockway Landing

The granite "elephant ledge" just past the southern end of Selden Creek marks the beginning of the industrious Brockway Landing community, extending south to Joshua Creek. From 1724 until the 1880s, William Brockway's ferry ran across to the cranberry bog in Deep River. The Brockway family built both 18th-century homes near the ledge (between the houses was John Ely's coopering shop). Just down the riverbank, Brockway's Shipyard averaged a large vessel per year from 1795 through the 1820s, including ships for the Stonington Antarctic sealing trade and two square-rigged brigs that made the 10,000-mile voyage to Cape Horn in 1820–21.

Oakum

Dominating the Brockway Landing settlement was the 100-foot brick smokestack of the Connecticut Oakum Company's mill. Oakum, the loose fiber from recycled ropes combined with tar, traditionally was used for caulking the seams of ships. At the mill, sheets of oakum were made for hospital use, much of it sold to New York's Bellevue Hospital. The two-foot by four-foot oakum sheets were reputed "to relieve the croup within fifteen minutes." The mill burned in 1888, but its smokestack stood fast until the 1938 hurricane.

The Egyptian lotus flower of the Nile

In 1878, an Essex doctor hunting in Selden Cove noticed a non-native lily with huge pads and gigantic 10-inch-high purplish-white flowers. The plant was identified as the Egyptian lotus flower of the Nile—a truly exotic species that purportedly bloomed on a 25 year cycle. In the 1850s, the Hartford Tool & Dye Company was importing linen and cotton from abroad, including from Egypt. Bales were off loaded at Essex, where wind and tides could have carried the lotus seeds to Selden Creek. The lily bloomed once more, in 1903. It is thought to have been washed away in the Great Flood of 1927.

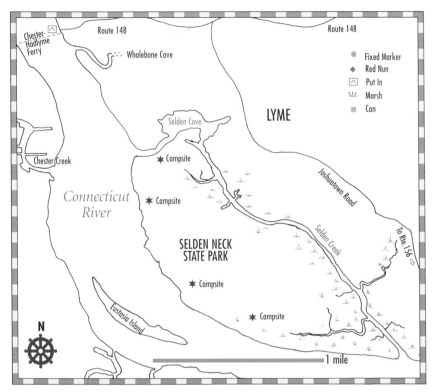

Selden Creek Access Table

Access Point
Adjacent to the Chester-Hadlyme Ferry landing, Route 148, 1.7 miles west of Hadlyme-Four Corners junction with Route 82.

Guidelines
Gillette Castle State Park, Connecticut DEP, Town of Lyme, unpaved parking for 20 cars.

Off the Ramp Directions
Paddle left down mainstream Connecticut River past Whalebone Cove.
Travel the river for another .9 mile, then left into Selden Cove.

Water/Marsh Type
Freshwater tidal marsh

Distance from Lynde Point Lighthouse
9.4 miles

Tidal Range
Mean 2.8 feet / highest tidal range 3.2 feet

Nearest Store
Hadlyme General Store, 3.3 miles up Route 148

Notes
For paddlers, getting to Selden Creek from the put-in at the Chester-Hadlyme Ferry landing can be made difficult by southwest winds blowing across the long expanse of water from Pratt Cove. Strong paddlers shouldn't have much difficulty, but inexperienced ones should note the winds before setting out. Watch for the ferry crossing.
The creek itself is a peaceful haven and is quite easy paddling.

Chapter 13

PRATT AND POST COVES, DEEP RIVER

CASUAL VISITORS to the lower Connecticut River are probably unaware of Pratt and Post coves. But hidden away off Essex Street are these two significant coves, the pride of the Deep River Land Trust, and the subject of extensive ecological studies sponsored by the Land Trust and The Nature Conservancy. These studies confirmed that these two coves have some of the most exemplary tidal freshwater marsh habitat in southern New England. A boating excursion to these coves is guaranteed to be memorable because of the rich plant community, the flocks of migratory birds, and the abundant fish population. You'll also be enthralled by the steam locomotive that passes by with its *chugga-chugga* sound and loud whistles. There is a car-top boat launch on Pratt Creek at the Essex Street Bridge.

The Essex Steam Train

The Essex Steam Train, powered by a 1920 steam engine, runs daily trips from its depot in Essex to the town dock on the Connecticut River in Deep River. From here, passengers can board the Deep River Navigation Company's excursion boats to take a delightful cruise on the river. The train and river tours are a very popular tourist attraction and a wonderful way to get acquainted with the area. Hearing and seeing the train gives you an opportunity to imagine what the river and coves may have been like a century ago.

A diverse plant community

Pratt and Post coves have not escaped development. In the 1800s, Pratt Creek was dredged and flatboats were used to deliver quarry stone to ships on the river for transport to New York and Boston. Today, there is a marina at the mouth of Pratt Creek. Despite the proximity of civilization, Pratt and Post coves are richly endowed with diverse plant communities. Large stands of wild rice and cattails provide food and cover to wildlife, while tapegrass and coontail provide cover for spawning and juvenile fish. Look, too, for large masses of pondweed—a vital food for mallards and black ducks. You'll notice the diversity of plants in Pratt Cove right from the put-in. Observe the zones of vegetation that dominate the flats and banks of Pratt Creek. On the mudflats, notice the common emergent plants of the freshwater intertidal community: spatter-dock, arrow-arum, and pickerelweed. And if you look away from the creek, a careful examination will reveal there's much more to these marshes than cattails. You'll find wild rice, sedges and rushes, jewelweed, and tearthumb (so named for the tiny rows of barbs on the stems), as well as shrubs like buttonbush and swamp rose.

Pratt Creek

Don't neglect exploring to the head of Pratt Cove. Pratt Creek snakes its way through the marsh, and each new bend affords an opportunity to spot a heron or egret stalking fish on the banks. In the late summer and early fall, waterfowl are abundant in the creek, and sometimes they'll surprise you by explosively taking flight. In the late summer, broad stands of wild rice in the coves feed large mixed flocks of red-winged blackbirds, common grackles, and song and swamp sparrows. Wood ducks, mallards, black ducks, green-winged teal, and soras also feed in the coves during migration. At any time but the dead of winter, you will likely hear the loud rattle of the belted kingfisher.

Approaching the river

When heading down the creek toward the Connecticut River, be wary of mute swans; they can be quite aggressive. Activity at the mouth of Pratt Creek is dominated by the hustle and bustle of Brewer's Marina. Much of the marina and adjacent land is on fill that was dumped in the marsh prior to the enactment of state and federal wetlands laws.

In the late 1990s, a major expansion was proposed for this marina. This caught the attention of local conservationists and the Connecticut River Watershed Council, which were concerned about adverse impacts on the tidal freshwater wetlands. The dispute ultimately led to a scaled-back expansion and some permanent protection for the coves.

As you approach the Connecticut, keep your head up and be aware of the powerboats around the marina. In fact, paddling north from Pratt Creek is not advised because of the marina traffic and, beyond, the steamboats docking at the town dock. From the mouth of Pratt Creek, paddle south along the shore and watch for ospreys that occasionally nest on the buoys in the river. Ospreys often feed on fish in the coves, diving after them in dramatic fashion with talons outstretched. In late summer, egrets disperse from breeding colonies on Long Island Sound for the coves of the lower river.

As you head south a short distance, you will come to the mouth of Post Cove, a long tidal creek that winds its way back to an expanse of marsh surrounded by private property. Both coves share very similar plant and animal communities, and both are just as wonderful to explore.

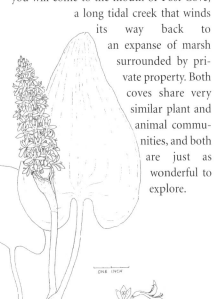

Pickerelweed
Art courtesy of Judy Preston

Elis Denison's shipyard c. 1866

Photo courtesy of Deep River Historical Society

Historical Notes

The ivory business

In 1809, George Read, abolitionist and a leading founder of Deep River, started an ivory business, initially making hand-cut ivory combs. Thirty years later, he began manufacturing ivory piano keys. Steamboats arriving at today's Town Landing (then called Saybrook Steamboat Dock) unloaded up to 12,000 pounds a month of elephant tusks from Zanzibar, and reloaded with cases of finished keyboards and other ivory products. It required 30 sunny days to dry the tusks in glass bleach houses. There's a reproduction of such a house behind the Deep River Historical Society.

Lace mill

Deep River's shipyards (primarily Denison's) built many vessels between 1793 and 1867. In 1905, Denison's sail loft became a lace mill, producing complex patterns for 85 years, after which its looms were dismantled and reassembled in France.

The renowned Captain Mather

Captain Samuel W. Mather was among the river's most renowned shipmasters. Although only in his mid-20s, Mather became famous by exploring new maritime routes and by setting speed records from Shanghai to London and from New York to Melbourne (1853) while at the helm of the clipper ship *Nightingale*.

Mount St. John

Mount St. John commands the summit of the hill above the Town Landing in Deep River. The fieldstone structure was built in 1907 by the Diocese of Hartford as an industrial school for boys. In 1919, it became an orphanage and then a boys' home. Today, it is a residential treatment center, an agency of the Diocese of Norwich, offering specific services to children who, for a variety of reasons, are unable to live at home.

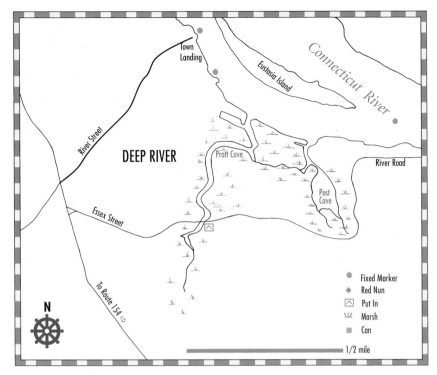

Pratt and Post Coves Access Table

Access Point
Route 9, exit 5, east on Route 80 .5 mile to Main Street (Route 154).
Right on Main one block, left on Essex Street .5 mile. Park on the right,
immediately after small bridge.

Guidelines
The Nature Conservancy public access, unpaved parking for 10 cars, car-top only.

Off the Ramp Directions
Take a right under the bridge out through Pratt Cove; paddle right down the Connecticut
River to Post Cove on the right.

Water/Marsh Type
Freshwater tidal marsh

Distance from Lynde Point Lighthouse
10.5 miles

Tidal Range
Mean 2.8 feet / highest tidal range 3.4 feet

Nearest Store
A number of stores and cafes are located in the village of Deep River on Route 154
about 2 miles away.

Notes
Paddling in Pratt and Post Coves is quite easy. There is little fetch, and the distance
of open river is nominal. Be wary, however, of the boating traffic at Brewer's
Marina in Deep River.

ONE INCH

Chapter 14

GREAT MEADOW,
NORTH COVE,
AND
FALLS RIVER COVE, ESSEX

THE LONG SHIPBUILDING history that began in the late 18th century is still reflected in the yacht clubs and boatyards that dominate the shores of Essex Village. But once you paddle into North Cove up along the Great Meadow, you'll leave behind the hum of boats and the gleam of elegant vessels. Instead, the *konk-la-ree* of redwinged blackbirds will fill your ears and the brilliance of yellow iris will catch your eye.

Setting Out

The best put-in for paddlers is at the Essex town park on Middle Cove. You can tell from the cove's shape that it's been dredged and enlarged for many years to accommodate

shipbuilding activities. From the put-in, you can paddle directly east out to the mainstream Connecticut, along the northern shore of Thatchbed Island, or head south through South Cove and explore the southern shores of the same island. In the winter, you'll find some American coots and ducks along Middle Cove, while summer boaters can listen for willow flycatchers and yellow warblers on Thatchbed Island. Both snowy and great egrets congregate along the flats on the river side of Thatchbed.

Connecticut River Museum

From Middle Cove, head north (by turning left) along the Essex waterfront.

Look for the Connecticut River Museum located on a former steamboat dock site. These docks once were dominated by ships delivering raw tusks of ivory for the manufacture of piano keys, billiard balls, and combs in Ivoryton and Centerbrook. The Museum is housed in an 1878 steamboat warehouse and offers permanent and changing exhibitions on the maritime, economic, and cultural history of the Connecticut River valley. The museum is open Tuesday through Sunday, from 10:00 A.M. to 5:00 P.M. (adult admission is $4.00, children $2.00). Members of the museum have docking privileges. There, one can visit the only full-scale working reproduction of the *American Turtle*, the first submarine built as a "secret weapon" to win the Revolutionary War. Common terns are often seen off the waterfront; listen for their raspy *kip-keeer* calls.

Essex Island

After passing the museum, depending on conditions, it's advisable to continue upriver along Essex Island (marina traffic poses a challenge to turning directly left into North Cove). In the winter, there are often bald eagles roosting there. The paddler will soon come to a shallow cut between the island and the Great Meadow that allows access to North Cove. Caution: the cut can prove challenging in a falling tide. Since North Cove has silted in and is quite shallow at low tide, you should time your trip to coincide with high tide. Essex is typically the northern limit of brackish water—a mix of salty Long Island Sound waters and the fresh surface waters of the Connecticut River. The brackish nature of the water, however, does vary according to the flows of the river. Saltwater is denser than freshwater and therefore extends along the bottom of the river much farther upstream than Essex (the so-called "salt wedge"). During the spring, when river flows from the watershed are at their peak from snowmelt and spring rains, all saltwater is flushed from the lower river. However, during the low flow periods late in the summer, the strength of the tides mixes saltwater farther upstream, well past Essex.

Great Meadow

If there is enough water, continue along the inside of Great Meadow. The taller narrow-leaved cattail dominates these brackish settings. However, as with other coves in the lower river, *Phragmites* is invading the marsh at an alarming rate. Also, look for false indigo and rose mallow in these areas. The extensive marshes of Great Meadow were an important source of marsh hay, once used as bedding for livestock. Several early settlers owned strips of the meadows for hay—still reflected on parcel maps of the area. Today, Great Meadow is an interesting brackish wetland community that is home to the Virginia rail, a secretive bird that is usually detected only by either its repetitive *ki-dik* or comical trumpeting call. An inventory of birds of the Essex shoreline found that Virginia rails commonly use Great Meadow as a nesting site. These birds are nocturnal, so they may possibly be seen at dawn and dusk.

North Cove and Falls River Cove

The ospreys that nest by the windmill are perhaps the most prominent birds in North Cove. Remember to steer clear of nesting ospreys to reduce the risk of exposing eggs by flushing a parent from the nest. Over by the meadows, listen for the *fitz-bew* of the willow flycatcher and the rattling song of the marsh wren. In the northern reaches of North Cove, look for Falls River Cove off to the left. This cove displays the diverse plant community of a true freshwater tidal cove. Pickerelweed and arrow-arum become more prevalent on the mudflats, while pondweed and tapegrass are the dominant aquatic plants. Falls River Cove and the Falls River are spawning grounds for migratory fish. In the spring, thousands of alewives return to these waters to spawn after spending about four years in Long Island Sound and the Atlantic Ocean. Restoration efforts along tributaries like Falls River have added tens of thousands of these fish to the lower-river ecosystem. Luckily, the dam at the head of the cove has been breached, allowing fish to make their way upstream to historical spawning areas. It's easy to

Essex Steam Train approaching Deep River

forget the time when exploring the North and Falls River coves. Be sure to head back before the tide gets too low; otherwise, the mudflats could become a difficult obstacle to overcome. Also, remember to steer clear of the osprey platform on the western shore.

Historical Notes

Essex ships and shipyards

Noah Tooker first built vessels in Essex in 1731. In 1776, the Connecticut Colony's first warship was constructed at Uriah Hayden's Dauntless Yard, extending along the riverfront from the foot of Main Street south to today's Essex Yacht Club. The 24-gun, 300-ton *Oliver Cromwell* captured nine British vessels before being captured herself in 1779. By the advent of the War of 1812, 35 years after the *Oliver Cromwell* was built, the town boasted seven sawmills and four grist mills, seven blacksmith shops, 113 pleasure carriages, and a 900-foot ropewalk (a long covered walk where ropes are manufactured). There were four major shipbuilding yards: the Dauntless Yard, the largest, by then owned by Richard Hayden; Calvin Hayden's yard on Mack Lane; and Samuel Williams's two North Cove yards, at Falls River and at the foot of New City Street.

The invasion of Essex

Early on April 8, 1814, 136 British marines led by Captain Richard Coote rowed six longboats up the ice-cluttered river to Essex. Arriving at 3:30 A.M., they burned 28 vessels, sunk the ship *Osage* at the Williams's Falls River yard, and left at 10:00 A.M. with the just-completed schooner *Black Prince* and the brig *Anaconda* in tow.

The Lyme and Killingworth militias, shooting from both sides of the river, killed two marines and forced Captain Coote to abandon and burn his booty.

The Essex Turnpike

Ely's Ferry began crossing from Lyme to midpoint on Essex's Great Meadow. Passengers, horse-drawn carriages, and oxcarts then struggled up Great Meadow's cobblestone ramp landing, traveled south on a dirt road, and crossed over a wooden drawbridge to reach Ferry Street in Essex Village. Incorporated as the Essex Turnpike in 1822, this section formed an important link on the northern Post Road, an alternate route between Boston and New York.

Ely's Ferry, landing, and tavern

Steamboats were a familiar sight along the river from 1822 to 1931. Visible upriver and on the opposite shore from the Connecticut River Museum (formerly Essex's steamboat dock and warehouse) is the small red freight house (circa 1840) at Ely's Ferry—all that remains of the once-busy Ely's Landing. Gone are its steamboat dock, warehouses, store, and William Ely's 24-room mansion, which later became a tavern. Both Daniel Webster and President Andrew Jackson stopped there.

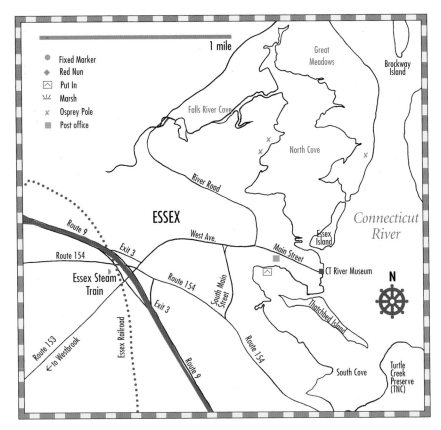

Great Meadow Access Table

Access Point
Route 9, exit 3. From the north, left off ramp onto Route 154, under bridge, left at light onto West Avenue. From the south, left off ramp onto Route 154, right at light onto West Avenue to Essex Center. Turn right into Post Office parking lot to ramp.

Guidelines
Car-top only, parking for about 10 cars.

Off the Ramp Directions
Paddle out of Middle Cove, then left upriver past Connecticut River Museum and Essex Island then left into North Cove.

Water/Marsh Type
Brackish tidal marsh

Distance from Lynde Point Lighthouse
6.5 miles

Tidal Range
Mean 3.0 feet / highest tidal range 3.6 feet

Nearest Store
Essex Village has several delis, cafes, and restaurants.

Notes
Generally easy with few real concerns. There is heavy boating use in the area. Be courteous to other boaters. North Cove is boatable only during high tides. High or low tide at Essex is 28 minutes after tide table listing for Old Saybrook Jetty.

Chapter 15

LORD COVE, OLD LYME

WHILE SEVERAL OF THE COVES of the Tidewaters can be accessed by road or by foot, a boat is necessary to truly appreciate Lord Cove. Its many creeks provide access to the cove's far reaches. Its size and abundant wildlife place Lord Cove as one of the premier habitats in the entire lower river. Because it's so large, Lord Cove is one of the few places where you can get turned around and become temporarily lost. Bring a compass just in case you do, as this is one cove where the map and site description will help only so much.

Setting Out

The very small parking area at Pilgrim's Landing off Route 156 demands courtesy and economy, so park efficiently. If you have two cars, park one in the commuter lot at I-95 and carpool up to the put-in. During duck hunting season (from early October on) this small area is frequently full early in the morning, although many of the hunters will leave by midday. Paddling during hunting season will include the sounds of shotguns from patient hunters in their blinds. It is wise to go during midday and to wear an orange or red hat or vest during hunting season.

Cattail and *Phragmites*

Lord Cove is dominated by narrow-leaved cattail, which is more tolerant of brackish water than the common cattail. Various animals use these cattails as nesting (for instance, marsh wrens) and as denning material (such as muskrats). The seeds and the stems are used by many as a food source.

Unfortunately, *Phragmites* or common reed is threatening Lord Cove; aerial photographs reveal large stands of this invasive pest. The Nature Conservancy, the U.S. Fish Wildlife Service, and the Connecticut Department of Environmental Protection are working jointly to stem the expansion of *Phragmites* in Lord Cove.

Calves Island and Goose Island

Head north from the put-in on the east side of Calves Island. Check the trees on Calves Island for roosting ospreys, herons, and egrets. Be aware: the area between Calves Island and the shore can have strong tides. As you approach the entrance to Lord Cove, the marsh on the left is Goose Island. *Phragmites* is quite extensive here. Goose Island was ditched for mosquito control decades ago, which may have contributed to the dominance of *Phragmites* today. You can often see egrets along the shore.

Wildlife

The area at the mouth of Lord Cove can be a good spot to observe menhaden (also known as bunkers) as bluefish chase them in the late summer. Occasionally, whole schools of fish will be chased literally out of the water.

Lord Cove is a place to get a sense of how food chains work, not just among fish species, but also among fishes, birds, and mammals. Least and common terns, herons, and egrets forage extensively on the cove's abundant killifish and silversides. Mink, otter, and raccoon use these marshes to forage for fish. Mink are surprisingly common along the lower river. They prey on small mammals, crustaceans, nesting birds, and in the freshwater portions, amphibians. Mink are especially wary (after all, they've been trapped for generations), and so only quiet and patient boaters will be rewarded with a view of one. Otters are much less common, but are still seen occasionally.

Ducks, swans, and *"rarae aves"*

In the fall, before hunting season, Lord Cove is one of the best locations in Connecticut to see marsh ducks, including black ducks, green-and blue-winged teal, and mallards. Open-water areas of the cove are sometimes filled with hundreds of ducks. In the summer, this very same area often supports dozens of mute swans, a beautiful but unwanted visitor. These aggressive non-native birds compete with native species for food and space. They tear up submerged grasses by the roots to forage, thereby damaging the cove's ecosystem. Their numbers continue to increase throughout the Tidewaters. In Lord Cove you can see nesting marsh birds that have become quite rare in Connecticut because of wetlands destruction. Both American and least bitterns have nested in Lord Cove (boaters in the cove just after dawn or dusk should listen for their strange pumping calls). The king rail, a very rare nester in Connecticut, has also been recorded nesting in Lord Cove. Virginia rails and soras are also common, although it is thought that the tidal fluctuations keep soras from being more abundant.

As you progress up the creek into Lord Cove, the oak and hickory forest along the steep eastern shore provides nesting habitat for forest birds. These woods can be alive with song in the spring as wood warblers, thrushes, and vireos establish their territories and seek their mates. Listen also for the more common nesting songbirds in the marsh, such as marsh wrens and red-winged blackbirds. In the late summer and early fall, Lord Cove becomes a theater for thousands of tree swallows. These aerialists often congregate or "stage" here late into the autumn. The warm waters of the cove create a

Common reed
Art courtesy of Judy Preston

ONE INCH

Lord Cove Aerial view

Side creeks

The Lord Cove's side creeks offer several options to the boater, and it's easy to lose your bearings. After continuing beyond Coults Hole, creeks lead off in a variety of directions. The upper reaches of the cove afford opportunities to observe nature's quiet pace and its glories. In recent years, bald eagles have brought excitement to the area. The northern harrier (marsh hawk) is a common resident in Lord Cove. Look for its characteristic low gliding flight over the cattails. In the fall, look for migrating Cooper's hawks and sharp-shinned hawks that prey on the cove's songbirds. Remember to keep track of the tides so that you will have an easy time getting home. The main section of Lord Cove can be quite shallow; mudflats appear at low tide. The tides will also affect your wildlife viewing. High tide floods force wildlife up into higher areas of the marsh. If possible, head up the cove with a rising tide and return on the falling tide.

warm haven for the insects on which they prey, and the marsh is an ideal roost.

Historical Notes

The ancient blackgum

Off the northwestern corner of Calves Island, a large dark stump is visible at very low tides. This is the ancient remnant of a blackgum tree, carbon-dated to be 1,400 years old (*circa* 600 A.D.). The tree was alive when sea levels were lower and today's river was still an alluvial floodplain. This attractive species, also called pepperidge, is still found today in other areas of the lower river.

Calves Island

From the 17th century until the 1920s, cows and their calves were ferried on scows from Pilgrim's Landing, south of the entrance to Lord Cove, to summer pasture on the island. Calves Island's 40 acres once were prized for their salt hay. In the late 1630s, Pequots attacked Lion Gardiner and two aides haying on the island. His aides allegedly fled, but Gardiner, though wounded in the leg by an arrow, made it back to the fort he had built on Saybrook Point.

The Black Prince *and the War of 1812*

When the British were retreating down the river after their April 1814 raid on the Essex shipyards, they were towing the barely completed, but still unballasted, 315-ton schooner *Black Prince,* which they had planned to use to further their own cause. But local militia fired on them from both sides of the river, forcing the British to scuttle their booty and burn the *Black Prince* off Calves Island.

Coults Hole

Coults Hole, located within the maze of marshland upstream from Lord Creek, perpetuates the name of the founder of an 18th-century farm east of Goose Island. The farm remained a working family operation until Billy Coult's death in 1940.

Cranberry picking

Lyme old-timers recall participating in the cranberry harvest in the bog at the head of Deep Creek, south of Ely's Ferry Road. The bog was protected by a stone dam and a gate that could be raised or lowered to control the water level. The gate was blown out by the hurricane of 1938, destroying the bog.

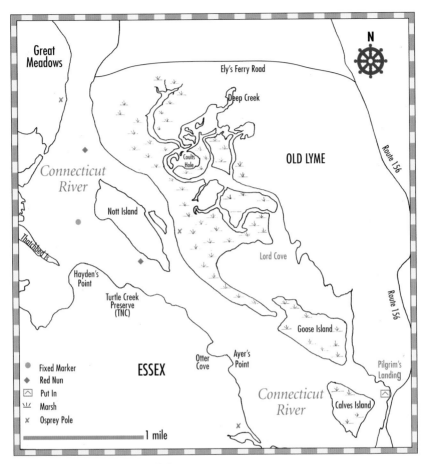

Lord Cove Access Table

Access Point
I-95, exit 70. Go north on Route 156 straight through lights past the marina. On the left is Pilgrim's Landing.

Guidelines
Town of Old Lyme public access, no permit required, limited unpaved parking, car-top only.

Off the Ramp Directions
Paddle north along the shoreline; bear right into Lord Cove to maze of creeks.

Water/Marsh Type
Brackish tidal marsh

Distance from Lynde Point Lighthouse
4.6 miles

Tidal Range
Mean 3.1 feet / highest tidal range 3.7 feet

Nearest Store
A&P at the Old Lyme Shopping Center.

Notes
Generally easy with few real concerns. However, in high winds, the broad expanses of marsh and open water can make paddling difficult. Some areas are quite shallow at low tide. In season, hunting is very popular, so be careful. Boating traffic on weekends can be quite high.

Chapter 16

LIEUTENANT RIVER, OLD LYME

PUTTING IN AT THE STATE BOAT launch at the Lieutenant River/Route 156 bridge presents the boater with two options. Boaters heading upstream will pass by waterfront homes, then under the I-95 and Hall's Road bridges. The Florence Griswold Museum is about a hundred yards farther on the right. Beyond, the upper Lieutenant River widens into a broad marsh joined by Mill Brook from the east.

Just passing through

In the spring, thousands of anadromous fish (migratory fishes that live in saltwater but spawn in freshwater) swim up the Connecticut and pass through these marshes to freshwater spawning areas upstream. Just as the first hatch of insects provides forage for migratory birds, these fish provide the forage base for a host of species throughout the marshes, the Connecticut River, and tributaries such as the Lieutenant River. Some researchers believe the restoration of anadromous fishes is of far-reaching environmental value. The Connecticut River Watershed Council is working with the State of Connecticut and local partners to restore these species to the Tidewaters.

These marshes represent a haven to spawning and young saltwater fishes that need a place to hide from larger predatory

Boating on the river

fish. Ocean species prevalent in these salt marshes include crevalle jack, winter flounder, and needlefish. In turn, these species provide a forage base for other fish like bluefish and menhaden and for birds such as osprey, terns, herons, and egrets. Notice that *Phragmites* has taken over the lower reaches of the marsh. This makes for a relatively uneventful ride on the mainstream Lieutenant, but it's worth exploring some of the nearby creeks and channels.

If the paddler heads downstream, a couple of choices are possible. Once you pass under the railroad bridge, the main stem of the Lieutenant bears right to its junction with the Connecticut River. From there, paddle up the Connecticut, under the railroad bridge to the DEP Marine Fisheries Headquarters at Ferry Landing State Park. Docks are available for day use at this popular picnic spot, and the interpretive signage along the boardwalk of the marsh provides interesting environmental education.

If it is high tide, another option is to turn left after passing under the railroad bridge, into a small creek. It brings you to the open backwaters of the Duck River, where you'll find shorebirds at the mudflats around Watch Rock (be careful not to get stuck in the mud!).

Art courtesy of Judy Preston

ONE INCH

Continuing south, you'll come out on the Back River leading to the Smith Neck state boat launch, described in the Griswold Point chapter.

Pannes and mosquitoes

Depressions in the salt marsh known as pannes provide important open water for birds and other species of wildlife in the marshes. Pannes often support widgeon grass and other plants that are important forage for ducks. Unfortunately, the channels dug back in the 1930s as mosquito control measures have altered the hydrology of these marshes so that fewer pannes form. The channels have also, some experts believe, aided the growth of *Phragmites*. The Connecticut Department of Environmental Protection's Mosquito Control Unit now promotes the formation of pannes and works to restore the natural functioning of the marshes and undo the damage caused by earlier mosquito control efforts. Late in the boating season these broad tidal areas support hundreds of ducks such as green-winged and blue-winged teal, mallards, and black ducks. Like shorebirds, ducks have come to rely on these areas as important rest stops during their migration. Some overwinter here. It's best not to disturb the birds if possible.

Aerial view of river traffic near Baldwin Bridge connecting Old Saybrook and Old Lyme

Historical Notes

The Hills and The Meteor

Lieutenant River shipbuilding began at Deming's Landing, near the bridge at Hall's Road, well before 1739, when the town authorized a 40-foot wharf just downstream from today's Ferry Road public landing. Samuel Hill's 1775 home, directly across the river from the public landing, is all that remains of Old Lyme's best-known yard. Samuel and his son Edward, both master shipwrights, built coastal-size vessels, many for the West Indies trade. Most could be floated out to the Connecticut River. But their largest, such as the 290-ton, 93-foot privateer *Meteor* built in 1813, had to be skidded overland along Ferry Road, an ancient Indian path.

Meat, soap, the news, and plumbing

Now a private residence, the first building on the northwest side of Ferry Road near the public landing was, in the 18th century, a butcher shop. It later became a soap factory, then offices of Old Lyme's first newspaper in the 1890s, and finally Speirs Plumbing Company until 1915.

The New London–New Haven trolley

In 1913, the predecessor of today's Route 156 bridge (over the Lieutenant River) carried track for the Shore Line Electric Railway Company's New London–New Haven trolley service. The two-and-a-half-hour ride cost 70 cents. Despite massive subsidies by Stonington multimillionaire Morton F. Plant, the line was too expensive to operate and was bedeviled by accident damage claims as well as by increasing competition from automobiles and trains. Trolley service never resumed after a strike in 1919.

The bells of Old Lyme

The steeple of Old Lyme's First Congregational Church is clearly visible from the river below the railroad bridge. When the original structure burned down, Colonel Charles Griswold brought plans from England for a London church by renowned architect Sir Christopher Wren. These plans were used to build a new church in 1816, which, unfortunately, was also destroyed by fire on Independence Day, 1907. To kick off the rebuilding fund, 500 small dinner bells were cast from the molten metal from the church's bells and sold at $1 each.

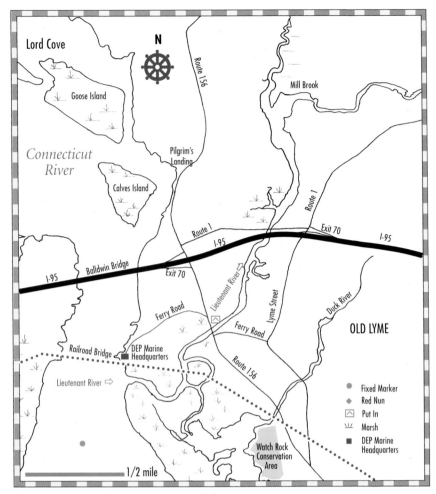

Lieutenant River Access Table

Access Point
I-95, exit 70. Go south .5 mile on Route 156.
Turn right into parking area just before the bridge over Lieutenant River.

Guidelines
Connecticut State DEP access, limited unpaved parking, car-top only.

Off the Ramp Directions
Paddle left under the bridge to go up the Lieutenant River, right to join the Connecticut at the DEP Marine Headquarters.

Water/Marsh Type
Brackish tidal marsh

Distance from Lynde Point Lighthouse
2.6 miles

Tidal Range
Mean 3.1 feet / highest tidal range 3.7 feet

Nearest Store
A&P at the Old Lyme shopping center.

Notes
High tide here is approximately 25 minutes later then the high tide at Lynde Point Lighthouse in Old Saybrook.

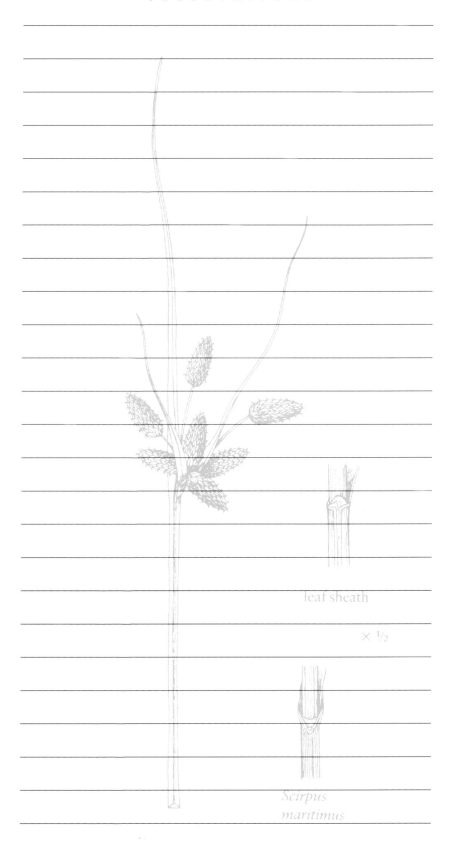

leaf sheath

× 1/2

Scirpus
maritimus

Art courtesy of David Dunlop

Chapter 17

RAGGED ROCK CREEK, OLD SAYBROOK

IMAGINE THE frustration of boaters traveling on Amtrak's New York to Boston line when they see the beautiful marshes of the lower Connecticut River as their train whisks them by. Ragged Rock Creek is one of those marshes. For boaters and explorers who observe the creek close up and at a leisurely pace, the train is an occasional jarring reminder that the world—and all its schedules—can't ever be completely forgotten.

Ecological richness

Ragged Rock Creek possesses some of the most exemplary salt and brackish marshes in the Tidewaters. A quiet visit to Ragged Rock Creek will remind you that the coves of the lower Connecticut are indeed special habitats that need careful stewardship. The stands of cord grass—which form the foundation of the ecological richness here—are represented by four separate species. The creek's relative seclusion contributes to its ecological value. Its shores serve as the nesting site for diamondback terrapins and as a roost site for black-crowned night herons.

Setting Out

Boating from the Baldwin Bridge boat launch can be difficult and offers little to observe until one actually reaches the marshes. From the boat launch, head down the river, hugging the west side, under the railroad trestle and then another three-quarters of a mile to the entrance of the creek. The fetch, boat wakes, and currents make observing difficult here. Be cautious of powerboats around the marinas and particularly around the railroad bridge, where the winds, currents, and waves are all a little trickier. Along this stretch of river, ospreys, great black-backed gulls, and double-crested cormorants are common. In recent years, the cormorant population on the river has exploded. Because cormorants are extremely efficient fish hunters, their increase is raising concerns among some biologists and commercial fishing interests.

Grasses

As you paddle downstream, keep an eye out for the mouth of the creek on the right. As you enter it, notice the different types of grasses there. In the low, frequently flooded areas, you can find smooth cord grass, the taller of the two dominant salt marsh grasses. Later on your journey, watch for the shorter salt meadow hay that dominates the high marsh. These two grasses indicate the high salinity of the water and the proximity of Long Island Sound. In the spring, very little saltwater makes its way upriver. However, in the late summer, when river flows are at their lowest, these marshes are much saltier, greater than 18 parts of salt per thousand parts of water. Ragged Rock Creek acts to restrict the incursion of saltwater. As you head up the creek, look for salt-reed grass; this plant is superficially similar to saltmarsh hay but occurs in brackish and fresh marshes. Farther up the creek, you might find yet another species of cord grass, freshwater cord grass, an indicator of still lower salinity.

Sharp-tailed sparrows

It is a true pleasure to journey up the serene and restful Ragged Rock Creek. Listen for salt marsh sharp-tailed sparrows; their song is a quiet *whoosh* often likened to escaping steam. These sparrows were formerly thought to be a subspecies, but have recently been given full species status by ornithologists. Their cup-nest made of coarse and fine grasses is well concealed in the salt marsh. Marsh wrens are abundant nesters here as well. Listen for their rapid, jumbled song. Pull up close to the marsh and just watch; a whole world will be revealed. Insects, amphipods, snails, spiders, and fiddler crabs both benefit from and contribute to the overwhelming productivity of the Ragged Rock Creek salt marsh.

Exploration routes

There are a couple of routes in and around Ragged Rock Creek. Staying right allows exploration of the upper reaches of the creek—up to where the rail line crosses the marsh. Veering immediately to the left after entering allows you to explore south toward North Cove in Old Saybrook. Occasionally, dead trees float into this channel and block the way to the cove, so be prepared: you may have to turn back. A number of smaller creeks allow quiet exploration of other portions of the marsh. In colder months, smaller creeks may afford a welcome break from the wind. However, in summer, the lack of wind allows no-see-ums and greenheads to attack. It is not uncommon to be driven out of a small creek by these aggressive flies.

Sandpipers and plovers

The main creek has wide mudflat margins that provide resting and feeding habitat to migratory shorebirds—sandpipers and plovers stopping to nest and refuel on their epic migrations to the tropics and beyond from nesting sites in the arctic tundra. Do not disturb them, since calories spent fleeing from boaters will be sorely missed on their trek south to the tropics and beyond.

Hunters: The food web

Killifish, mummichogs, and silversides form a fundamental link in the fish community of the creek. These fish feed on larval insects and zooplankton and, in turn, are prey for larger fish, terns, and herons. Occasionally, there are wonderful opportunities to observe the hunting styles of the bird predators. Snowy egrets' active stalking provides contrast to the slow, methodical hunting strategy of green herons. Double-crested cormorants chase the fish underwater and occasionally scare them literally out of the water. Belted kingfishers and common terns hover above the water only to plunge suddenly downward—more often than not, they come up with a fish. Menhaden, bluefish, and hickory shad hunt the killifish as well. They chase the minnows down with bursts of speed and group attacks. These fishes also feed on mullet. It's not uncommon to see a whole school of mullet or silversides suddenly shoot out of the water in an effort to escape from an unseen foe. Ragged Rock Creek is also an important spawning site for alewives and rainbow smelt.

Back home

The trip back to the boat ramp can be just as challenging as the trip to the creek. Be aware of the tides and, if you are fighting tide and

current, expect the return to take longer than the trip down. Somehow, though, after a quiet exploration of Ragged Rock Creek, the world—and all its schedules—seems a little less busy and pressing.

Railroad Station & Dock, Saybrook Point
Photo Courtesy of Old Saybrook Historical Society

Historical Notes

Pashbeshauke

The original inhabitants of the area, the Nehantic tribe, situated their fishing village at Saybrook Point. They named it Pashbeshauke, meaning "place at the river's mouth." From there, the peaceful Nehantics fished the waters of the river long before they were conquered by Pequots in 1590.

The smiling face

Only six years after Adriaen Block explored the "Long Tidal River" up to Wethersfield in 1614, traders from the Dutch West India Company were taking 10,000 beaver pelts a year in trading with the Indians. In 1635, Governor John Winthrop Jr. sent a small bark bearing twenty English carpenters and soldiers to claim jurisdiction under the Warwick Patent. Under its terms, fifteen Puritan "Lords and Gentlemen" were given the right by King James I to settle the entire area "from the Narragansett River west to the Pacific." The arriving British tore the Dutch coat of arms off the small trading post, set up two cannon, and erected a shield with a grinning face on it. The Dutch ship that approached a few days later withdrew on sighting the face and the cannon, and Holland's brief hegemony over the Connecticut River was over.

Lion Gardiner

Governor Winthrop renamed the point "Saybrook" in honor of two of the fifteen Patentee sponsors, Viscount Saye and Lord Brooke. The following spring, in 1636, Lion Gardiner, a skilled military engineer, built a

square fort at Saybrook Point with palisades, a moat, two wells, and cannon at each corner. (Those early earthworks were leveled around 1870 in order to construct the Connecticut Valley Railroad's turntable, roundhouse, and yards.) Gardiner's four-year contract had expired when Colonel George Fenwick arrived in 1639, and Gardiner retired with his family across Long Island Sound to the island that bears his name. The informative signage at Fort Saybrook Park and the remains of the fort and the railroad roundhouse are well worth a visit. The park is on the river, at the end of College Street (Route 154) at Saybrook Point.

The American Turtle

In the late summer of 1775, Benjamin Franklin traveled down the river, past Ragged Rock Creek, to observe water trials of America's first submarine, the *American Turtle*, invented by Saybrook's David Bushnell and piloted by a 27-year-old volunteer from Lyme, Captain Ezra Lee. The one-man vessel, whose torpedo was equipped with a timed bomb detonator, had been developed in deepest secrecy at Ayer's Point. The plan was to torpedo the 64-gun *Eagle*, flagship of the British naval squadron blockading New York harbor. Lee's daring pre-dawn raid in 1776 failed, as did his two subsequent attempts on British ships, but the mere presence of the tiny *Turtle* had struck terror into the entire enemy fleet. A replica is at the Connecticut River Museum in Essex.

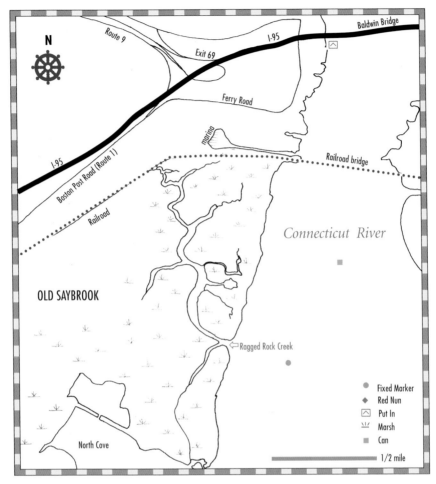

Ragged Rock Creek Access Table

Access Point
from west, take exit 67, I-95; (from east, take exit 69). Go east on Route 1.
Take a right on Ferry Road. The put-in is under Baldwin Bridge.

Guidelines
State DEP boat launch access, Town of Old Saybrook. Parking for 75 cars with trailers.
Cement ramp with pads. Crowded on weekend. You have to pay a fee.

Off the Ramp Directions
Paddle south down mainstream Connecticut River 1.25 miles, right into Ragged Rock Creek.

Water/Marsh Type
Brackish tidal marsh

Distance from Lynde Point Lighthouse
2 miles

Tidal Range
Mean 3.1 feet / highest tidal range 3.7 feet

Nearest Store
Cloud Nine, Route 1, close to Ferry Point Road and I-95 north ramp.

Notes
From the put-in at Baldwin Bridge to the mouth of the creek, wakes from large boats and
waves generated over long fetch create difficult boating on the main river. Also, be wary of
larger boat traffic, particularly around the marinas. Once in the creek the boating is easy.

Art courtesy of David Dunlop

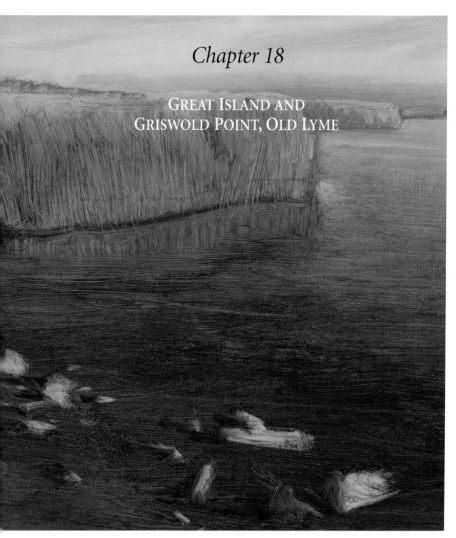

Chapter 18

GREAT ISLAND AND GRISWOLD POINT, OLD LYME

AT FIRST LOOK, the extensive salt marshes—known as Great Island—as seen from the Smith Neck boat launch seem to be little more than a monotonous stretch of grass. However, these salt and brackish marshes at the mouth of the Connecticut River are among the most significant estuarine habitats in the northeastern United States. These marshes and the beach-dune habitats of Griswold Point are home to some of the rarest species in the entire 11,260-square-mile watershed of the Connecticut River. Few boaters will fail to be impressed by the abundance of nesting ospreys, the subtle beauty of the salt marsh grasses, or the vast runs of schooling fishes.

Salt marsh productivity

In terms of sheer productivity, salt marshes are unrivaled—even by rainforests. This productivity is most obvious in the marsh grasses that dominate Great Island, and is augmented by the productivity of mud algae and aquatic phytoplankton. The sheer mass of plants, algae, and plankton provides the foundation for a tremendously rich community of microscopic bacteria and zooplankton that, in turn, feeds larger organisms—right on up to ospreys, striped bass, and humans.

Salt marsh peat

The incredible productivity of the salt marsh not only provides the foundation of the rich ecosystem, but also alters the actual physical structure through the accumulation of peat. The roots of older plants and the sheer volume of plant material, as well as sediments settling out from high tides, accumulate to form rich organic peat. The high channel walls of salt marsh creeks provide a chance to observe how this peat provides a habitat in its own right.

Ospreys

It is nearly impossible to visit this area and not see ospreys from March until late September. In many respects, the return of the ospreys parallels the return of the Connecticut River. Since the river has recovered from pollution, the harm caused decades ago by DDT has receded, and ospreys are once again abundant in these marshes. Actually, boaters now pose a greater risk to these majestic birds than do environmental contaminants. Please stay away from osprey platforms, and if you see an osprey leave a platform because you're too close, paddle away. The worst thing you can do is scare an osprey off its nest. That exposes the eggs to cooling or over-heating, and makes the eggs easy prey for gulls. The nesting platforms are quite visible, and it's easy and rewarding to observe ospreys from a distance.

Griswold Point

There are many options for boaters in this area. One of the nicest routes is to boat south from the Smith Neck launch to the inside of Griswold Point, get out to stretch, and perhaps look for the piping plovers that nest there (of course, keep your distance.) The species is listed as threat-ened under the federal Endangered Species Act, and much of Griswold Point is off limits during the early sum-mer nesting season. The Nature Conservancy hires a preserve steward every summer to monitor the popula-tion. These stewards often have a wealth of information about plovers and will be happy to talk with you about them. Be careful of the strong currents in

the channel at the end of Griswold Point.

Shifting sands

The dynamic nature of the area is reflected by the ever-changing geography of the point. The steady accumulation of sediments and sands along Griswold Point is occasionally disrupted by large storms that erode and shift the marshes. The cut that is now passable by kayak at high tide was opened in 1993 by a November storm. Interestingly, that cut also uncovered a nearly 200-year-old unidentified ship, the remains of which were washed away in a subsequent storm.

Mudflats

At low tide, there are extensive mudflats that support hundreds of feeding shorebirds during migration, such as greater and lesser yellowlegs, black-bellied plovers, and semipalmated sandpipers. Due to the timing of shorebird migrations, the mudflats support shorebirds through-out most of the summer. The latest north-bound migrant is here until mid-June, and the earliest southbound (post-breeding) shorebird can usually be expected in mid-July. The number of birds peaks toward the end of August. In the fall, keep your head up for migrating falcons; you might see one attempt to snare a shorebird. Most of the shorebirds encountered in this area are resting before continuing on their migrations, usually thousands of miles long. Please watch from a distance and give flocks space to rest and feed.

Phragmites once again

Boaters will also notice that there are large stands of taller marsh grass. This is *Phragmites* once again, the plant that is taking over areas of the marshes of the lower Connecticut River. Conservation groups are working on

Common salt marsh glasswort
Art courtesy of Judy Preston

PRESTON 95

limiting the further expansion of *Phragmites* in the Tidewaters.

Black Hall River

After checking out Griswold Point, it's fun to explore up the Black Hall River. The extensive salt hay marshes give way to a more diverse plant community after you go under the Route 156 bridge. As the salinity decreases, so does the salt stress and tidal fluctuation that limit the number of plant species competing for space in this habitat. The dominant plant changes from the saltmarsh hay to a narrow-leaved cattail that favors brackish settings. There are extensive tidal flats on the lower Black Hall, and shorebirds and snowy and great egrets are abundant here. Later in the fall, green-winged teal, mallards, and black ducks descend on the marshes to feed on algae and invertebrates. Look out for northern harriers coursing low with upturned wings over the marshes in search of voles or muskrats. It's possible to trace the progression from salt marsh to brackish to fresh along the Black Hall. Fortunately, the river has lately been the focus of conservation attention, and a significant amount of watershed land has been conserved here. Also, fishways have been installed on private land to increase the run of river herring, locally known as "buckies." Heading farther up the Black Hall River, the plant community gets much more diverse, with pickerelweed, arrowhead, and tapegrass becoming more prevalent. Also, dogwoods and maples encroach on the marsh, offering a perching area for kingfishers and a nesting area for yellow warblers.

Historical Notes

Lady Fenwick's Grave

Soon after Col. George Fenwick arrived in 1639 to head the Saybrook Colony, he brought stonecutter Matthew Griswold and his wife downriver from the Windsor settlement. Able and respected, Griswold soon became the Colonel's business agent. Sadly, Fenwick's wife, Lady Alice, died in childbirth in 1645. Matthew Griswold carved her gravestone and, that year, was granted title by the Colonel to the Black Hall-Griswold Point section of today's Old Lyme. In appreciation, Griswold promised that he and his heirs would visit her grave annually and maintain the gravesite in perpetuity. Lady Fenwick's stone casket is in Old Saybrook's Cypress Cemetery, and Griswold descendants continue to honor their ancestor's pledge.

Black or Block

The Griswold land grant was originally known as "Black's Hall." Conventional wisdom long held that Matthew Griswold built a hut for his black servant who lived on the point before 1650. But recent research suggests that "Black's Hall" more likely was a colonial English corruption of "Block's Hole." Dutch explorer Adriaen Block not only explored the Connecticut River in 1614, but also carefully charted the eastern coast, including Block Island. In the 17th century, Niantic's Black Point was known as "Block's Point." In marine terminology, a hole means a deep cove or body of water with strong currents caused by constricting pieces of land—as in the topography where the Black Hall River joins the Connecticut River at Griswold Point.

Poverty Island

During the 1930s, a man named Jerome lived in a sunken houseboat on Poverty Island, noted on today's topographical maps off the southwestern edge of Great Island. He owned that land, plus three small houses on stilts across the wide sandbar on Poverty Point (he rented out the houses in the summer). In 1931, when Neri Clark's father lost his factory job, he bought a section of Jerome's sandbar, on which he built a tiny fishing shack. He supported his family selling steamers, fish, and eels at Saybrook Point's market. Other people did the same. The great hurricane of 1938 destroyed the houseboats, houses, and shacks, and even Poverty Island itself.

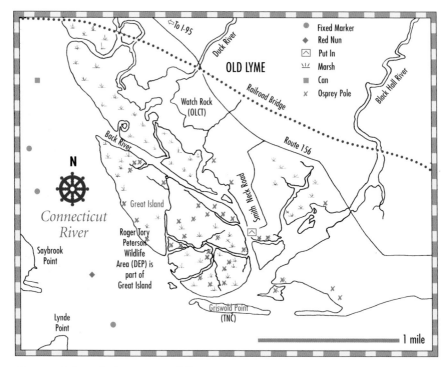

Great Island Access Table

Access Point

I-95, exit 70. Go south on Route 156 for 1 mile. Take a right on Smith Neck Road and follow it to its end (1.5 miles).

Guidelines

Connecticut DEP public boat launch. Parking for 30 cars with trailers, moderately used. Put in is shallow at low tide.

Off the Ramp Directions

Paddle south to Black Hall River on left, Griswold Point straight ahead. Turn north to Back River on left, cove on right.

Water/Marsh Type

Saltwater tidal marsh

Distance from Lynde Point Lighthouse

.6 mile

Tidal Range

Mean 3.2 feet / highest tidal range 4.2 feet

Nearest Store

A & P, Old Lyme shopping center

Notes

Generally easy, with few real concerns. However, in high, winds the broad expanses of salt marsh and open water can make paddling quite difficult. Strong tidal currents can also increase the difficulty of paddling in these areas — particularly at the tip of Griswold Point. Spring freshet flows can be prohibitively strong and can overwhelm the tidal fluctuations in this area. Boating traffic on weekends can be quite high.

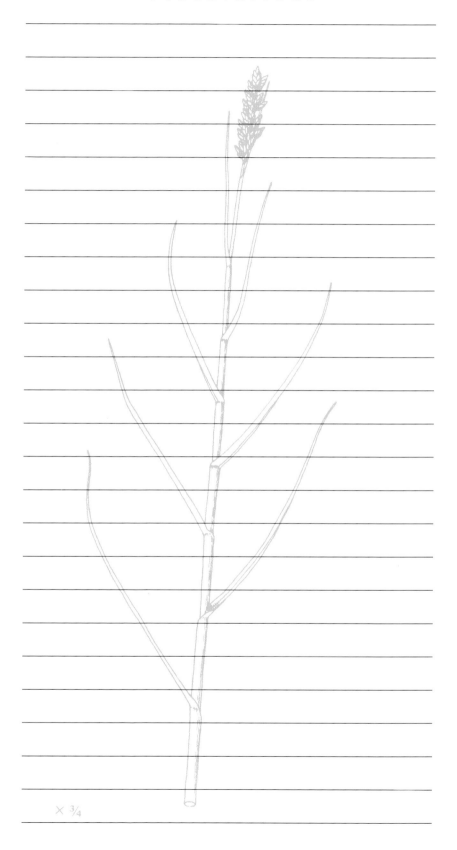

× ¾

Connecticut River Animal Species Checklist

THE FOLLOWING CHECKLISTS contain the common and latin names of the animals and plants discussed in this book. Although the bulk of commonly found species are listed, these lists are not meant to be the definitive Connecticut River species list. Note: *family names non-italics*

INVERTEBRATES

- [ ] giant bryozoan *Pectinatella magnifica*
- [ ] oligochaete worm *Limnodrilus hoffmeisteri*

INSECTS

- [ ] backswimmers Notonectidae*
- [ ] black flies Simuliidae
- [ ] broad-winged skipper *Poanes viator*
- [ ] caddisflies Trichoptera
- [ ] craneflies Tipulidae
- [ ] crawling water beetles Haliplidae
- [ ] damselflies Zygoptera
- [ ] deerflies Tabanidae
- [ ] diving beetles Dytiscidae
- [ ] dobsonflies Corydalidae
- [ ] dragonflies Anisoptera
- [ ] giant water bugs Belostomatidae
- [ ] grasshoppers Acrididae
- [ ] greenhead fly *Tabanus nigrovittatus*
- [ ] ground crickets Gryllidae: Nemobiinae
- [ ] honeybee *Apis mellifera*
- [ ] mantids Mantidae: *Mantis religiosa, Tenodera aridifolia*
- [ ] mayflies Ephemeroptera
- [ ] meadow katydids Tettigoniidae: Conocephalinae
- [ ] midges Chironomidae
- [ ] monarch *Danaus plexippus*
- [ ] punkies Ceratopogonidae
- [ ] puritan tiger beetle *Cicindela puritana*
- [ ] red admiral *Vanessa atalanta*
- [ ] robber flies Asilidae
- [ ] salt marsh dragonfly *Erythrodiplax berenice*
- [ ] salt marsh mosquito *Aedes* spp.
- [ ] sand flies Psychodidae
- [ ] stoneflies Plecoptera
- [ ] tiger swallowtail *Papilio glaucus*
- [ ] water boatmen Corixidae
- [ ] waterlily leaf beetles Chrysomelidae
- [ ] water measurers or marsh treaders Hydrometridae
- [ ] water penny beetles Psephenidae
- [ ] water scavenger beetle Hydrophilidae
- [ ] water scorpions Nepidae
- [ ] water striders Gerridae
- [ ] whirligig beetles Gyrinidae

SPIDERS

- [ ] fishing spiders *Dolomedes* spp.
- [ ] wolf spiders *Pardosa* spp.

- [ ] barnacles Cirripedia
- [ ] blue crab *Callinectes sapidus*
- [ ] crayfish Cambaridae
- [ ] green crab *Carcinus maenas,*
- [ ] mud fiddler crab *Uca pugnax*
- [ ] red-jointed fiddler crab *Uca minax*
- [ ] sand fiddler crab *Uca pugilator*
- [ ] sand shrimp *Crangon septemspinosa*
- [ ] shore shrimps *Palaemonetes* spp.

- [ ] alewife floater *Anodonta implicata*
- [ ] asiatic clam *Corbicula fluminea*
- [ ] chinese mystery snail *Cipangopaludina chinensis*
- [ ] dwarf wedgemussel *Alasmidonta heterodon*
- [ ] eastern elliptio *Elliptio complanata*
- [ ] eastern lampmussel *Lampsilis radiata*
- [ ] eastern pondmussel *Ligumia nasuta*
- [ ] fingernail clams Sphaeriidae
- [ ] marsh snail *Melampus bidentatus*
- [ ] mud snail *Ilyanassa obsoleta*
- [ ] piedmont elimia *Elimia virginica*
- [ ] ribbed mussel *Geukensia demissa*
- [ ] tidewater mucket *Lampsilis ochracea*
- [ ] triangle floater *Alasmidonta undulata*
- [ ] yellow lampmussel *Lampsilis cariosa*
- [ ] zebra mussel *Dreissena polymorpha*

- [ ] diamondback terrapin *Malaclemys terrapin*
- [ ] northern water snake *Nerodia sipedon*
- [ ] painted turtle *Chrysemys picta*
- [ ] snapping turtle *Chelydra serpentina*

- [ ] american toad *Bufo americanus*
- [ ] bullfrog *Rana catesbeiana*
- [ ] gray treefrog *Hyla versicolor*
- [ ] green frog *Rana clamitans*
- [ ] mudpuppy *Necturus maculosus*
- [ ] northern leopard frog *Rana pipiens*
- [ ] pickerel frog *Rana palustris*
- [ ] spring peeper *Pseudacris crucifer*

- [ ] alewife *Alosa pseudoharengus*
- [ ] american shad *Alosa sapidissima*
- [ ] atlantic silverside *Menidia menidia*
- [ ] atlantic sturgeon *Acipenser oxyrinchus*
- [ ] banded killifish *Fundulus diaphanus*
- [ ] blueback herring *Alosa aestivalis*
- [ ] bluefish *Pomatomus saltatrix*
- [ ] central mudminnow *Umbra limi*

- [ ] gizzard shad *Dorosoma cepedianum*
- [ ] largemouth bass *Micropterus salmoides*
- [ ] menhaden *Brevoortia tyrannus*
- [ ] mummichog *Fundulus heteroclitus*
- [ ] northern pike *Esox lucius*
- [ ] sheepshead minnow *Cyprinodon variegatus*
- [ ] shortnose sturgeon *Acipenser brevirostrum*
- [ ] spottail shiner *Notropis hudsonius*
- [ ] striped bass *Morone saxatilis*
- [ ] striped killifish *Fundulus majalis*

- [ ] bittern, American *Botarus lentiginosus*
- [ ] bittern, least *Ixobrychus exilis*
- [ ] blackbird, red-wing *Agelaius phoeniceus*
- [ ] bufflehead *Bucephala albeola*
- [ ] catbird, gray *Dumetella carolinensis*
- [ ] cormorant, double-crested *Phalacrocorax auritus*
- [ ] cormorant, great *Phalacrocorax carbo*
- [ ] dowitcher, short-billed *Limnodromus griseus*
- [ ] duck, American black *Anas rubripes*
- [ ] duck, wood *Aix sponsa*
- [ ] dunlin *Calidris alpina*
- [ ] eagle, American bald *Haliaeetus leucocephalus*
- [ ] eagle, golden *Aquila chrysaetos*
- [ ] egret, great *Ardea alba*
- [ ] egret, snowy *Egretta thula*
- [ ] falcon, peregrine *Falco peregrinus*
- [ ] gannet, northern *Morus bassanus*
- [ ] goldeneye, common *Bucephala clangula*
- [ ] goose, Canada *Branta canadensis*
- [ ] grebe, red-necked *Podiceps grisegena*
- [ ] gull, greater black-backed *Larus marinus*
- [ ] gull, herring *Larus argentatus*
- [ ] gull, ring-billed *Larus delawarensis*
- [ ] harrier, northern *Circus cyaneus*
- [ ] hawk, Cooperís *Accipiter cooperii*
- [ ] hawk, red-shouldered *Buteo linaetus*
- [ ] hawk, red-tailed *Buteo jamaicensis*
- [ ] hawk, rough-legged *Buteo lagopus*
- [ ] hawk, sharp-shinned *Accipter striatus*
- [ ] heron, great blue *Ardea herodias*
- [ ] heron, green *Butorides striatus*
- [ ] killdeer *Charadrius vociferus*
- [ ] kingfisher, belted *Ceryle alcyon*
- [ ] loon, common *Gavia immer*
- [ ] loon, red-throated *Gavia stellata*
- [ ] mallard *Anas platyrhynchos*
- [ ] merganser, common *Mergus merganser*
- [ ] merganser, red-breasted *Mergus serrator*
- [ ] nuthatch, white-breasted *Sitta carolinensis*
- [ ] oriole, Baltimore *Icterus galbula*

- [ ] osprey *Pandion haliateus*
- [ ] owl, short-eared *Asio flammeus*
- [ ] oystercatcher, American *Haematopus palliates*
- [ ] plover, black-bellied *Pluvialis squatarola*
- [ ] plover, semipalmated *Charadrius semipalmatus*
- [ ] rail, clapper *Rallus longirostris*
- [ ] rail, king *Rallus elegans*
- [ ] rail, Virginia *Rallus limicola*
- [ ] sandpiper, least *Calidris minutella*
- [ ] sandpiper, semipalmated *Calidris pusilla*
- [ ] sandpiper, spotted *Actitus macularia*
- [ ] sora *Porzana carolina*
- [ ] sparrow, savannah *Passerculus sandwichensis*
- [ ] sparrow, seaside *Ammodramus maritimus*
- [ ] sparrow, sharp-tailed *Ammodramus caudacutus*
- [ ] sparrow, song *Melospiza melodia*
- [ ] sparrow, swamp *Melospiza georgiana*
- [ ] swallow, tree *Iridoprocne bicolor*
- [ ] swan, mute *Cygnus olor*
- [ ] tanager, scarlet *Piranga olivacea*
- [ ] teal, blue-winged *Anas disors*
- [ ] teal, green-winged *Anas crecca*
- [ ] tern, common *Sterna hirundo*
- [ ] tern, least *Sterna antillarum*
- [ ] titmouse, tufted *Baeolophus bicolor*
- [ ] towhee, Eastern *Pipilo erythrophthalmus*
- [ ] vireo, red-eyed *Vireo olivaceus*
- [ ] vireo, white-eyed *Vireo griseus*
- [ ] vulture, turkey *Cathartes aura*
- [ ] warbler, hooded *Wilsonia citrina*
- [ ] warbler, worm-eating *Helmitheros vermivora*
- [ ] warbler, yellow *Dendroica petechia*
- [ ] willet *Catoptrophorus semi palmatus*
- [ ] wren, marsh *Cistothorus palustris*
- [ ] yellowlegs, greater *Tringa melanoleucus*
- [ ] yellowlegs, lesser *Tringa flavipes*
- [ ] yellowthroat, common *Geothlypis trichas*

MAMMALS
- [ ] beaver *Castor canadensis*
- [ ] harbor seal *Phoca vitulina*
- [ ] meadow vole *Microtus pennsylvanicus*
- [ ] mink *Mustela vison*
- [ ] muskrat *Ondatra zibethica*
- [ ] raccoon *Procyon lotor*
- [ ] star-nosed mole *Condylura cristata*
- [ ] white-tailed deer *Odocoileus virginianus*

Connecticut River Vegetative Species Checklist

- [ ] arrow-arum *Peltandra virginica*
- [ ] arrowleaf *Sagittaria graminea* and *S. latifolia*
- [ ] arrow-wood *Viburnum recognitum*
- [ ] bedstraws *Galium palustre, G. obtusum, G. tinctorium*

- [ ] beggar's-tick *Bidens,* spp.
- [ ] big cord-grass *Spartina cynosuroides*
- [ ] black grass *Juncus gerardii*
- [ ] blue flag *Iris versicolor, I. prismatica*
- [ ] boneset *Eupatorium perfoliatum*
- [ ] bulrushes *Scirpus pedicillatus* and *S. validus*
- [ ] bur-marigolds *Bidens laevis, B. cernua*
- [ ] cardinal flower *Lobelia cardinalis*
- [ ] cattails hybrid of *Typha angustifolia* and *Typha glauca*
- [ ] clearweeds *Pilea fontana* and *P. pumila*
- [ ] climbing hempweed *Mikania scandens*
- [ ] common beggar's-tick *Bidens frondosa*
- [ ] common cattail *Typha latifolia*
- [ ] common elderberry *Sambucus canadensis*
- [ ] common reed *Phragmites australis*
- [ ] common sneezeweed *Helanium autumnale*
- [ ] common three-square *Scirpus pungens*
- [ ] coontail *Ceratophyllum demersum*
- [ ] creeping bent *Agrostis stolonifera,* variety, *palustris*
- [ ] ditch moss *Elodea canadensis* and *Eleocharis nuttalii*
- [ ] eastern lilaeopsis *Lilaeopsis chinensis*
- [ ] estuarine bulrush *Scirpus cylindricus*
- [ ] false indigo *Amorpha fruticosa*
- [ ] false nettle *Boehmeria cylindrica*
- [ ] false pimpernel *Lindernia dubia*
- [ ] forget-me-not *Myosotis scorpoides*
- [ ] freshwater cord grass *Spartina pectinata*
- [ ] germander *Teucrium canadensis*
- [ ] glasswort *Salicornia europaea*
- [ ] golden-pert *Gratiola aurea*
- [ ] green-threads *Enteromorpha* spp.
- [ ] groundnut *Apios americana*
- [ ] groundsel tree *Baccharis halimifolia*
- [ ] honeysuckles *Lonicera morrowii, L. japonica*
- [ ] horned pondweed *Zannichellia palustris*
- [ ] Japanese stilt grass *Microstegium viminium*
- [ ] Joe-pye weed *Eupatorium dubium*
- [ ] marsh elder *Iva frutescens*
- [ ] marsh fern *Thelypertis palustris*
- [ ] marsh-purslane *Ludwigia palustris*
- [ ] marsh Saint Johnswort *Hypericum virginicum*
- [ ] meadow-sweet *Spiraea latifolia*
- [ ] mud-purslanes *Elatine americana* and *E. minima*
- [ ] northern swamp buttercup *Ranunculus septontrionalis*
- [ ] orach *Atriplex patula*
- [ ] pickerelweed *Pontedaria cordata*
- [ ] poison ivy *Toxicodendron radicans*
- [ ] pondweed *Potamogeton* spp.
- [ ] purple loosestrife *Lythrum salicaria*
- [ ] rattlesnake grass *Glyceria canadensis*
- [ ] redtop *Festuca rubra*
- [ ] reed bentgrass *Calamagrostis canadensis*

- [ ] regal fern *Osmunda regalis*
- [ ] rice-cutgrass *Leersia oryzoides*
- [ ] river bulrush *Scirpus fluviatilis*
- [ ] river sedge *Carex lacustris*
- [ ] rose-mallow *Hibiscus palustris*
- [ ] sago pondweed *Polygonum pectinatus*
- [ ] salt marsh aster *Aster tenuifolius*
- [ ] salt marsh bulrush *Scirpus maritime*
- [ ] salt marsh fleabane *Pluchea purpurascens*
- [ ] salt marsh plantain *Plantago oliganthos*
- [ ] salt marsh sand-spurrey *Spergularia marina*
- [ ] salt meadow hay *Spartina patens*
- [ ] sea lavender *Limonium nashii*
- [ ] sea lettuce *Ulva lactuca*
- [ ] seaside gerardia *Agalinis maritima*
- [ ] seaside goldenrod *Solidago sempervirens*
- [ ] sedge *Carex hormathodes*
- [ ] seedbox *Ludwigia alterniflora*
- [ ] sensitive fern *Onoclea sensibilis*
- [ ] silky dogwood *Cornus ammomum*
- [ ] silverweed *Potentilla anserina*
- [ ] skullcaps *Scutellaria epilobiifolia* and *S. lateriflora*
- [ ] smartweeds *Polygonum lapthifolium, P. punctatum*
- [ ] smooth cord grass *Spartina alterniflora*
- [ ] speckled alder *Alnus rugosa*
- [ ] spike-rush *Eleocharis rostellata*
- [ ] spike-rushes *Eleocharis* spp.
- [ ] spotted touch-me-not *Impatiens capensis*
- [ ] swamp-candles *Lysimachia terrestris*
- [ ] swamp rose *Rosa palustris*
- [ ] sweetflag *Acorus calamus*
- [ ] switchgrass *Panicum virgatum*
- [ ] tapegrass *Vallisneria americana*
- [ ] tear-thumbs *Polygonum arifolium, P. sagittatum*
- [ ] three-way sedge *Dulichium arundinaceum*
- [ ] tussock sedge *Carex stricta*
- [ ] virgin's bower *Clematis virginiana*
- [ ] water-hemlock *Cicuta bulbifera*
- [ ] water-horehounds *Lycopus uniflorus, L. americanus, L. virginicus*
- [ ] water horsetail *Equisetum fluviatile*
- [ ] water-lilies *Nymphaea odorata*
- [ ] water milfoil *Myriophyllum spicatum*
- [ ] water-pepper *Polygonum hydropiperoides*
- [ ] water pimpernel *Samolus parviflorus*
- [ ] water stargrass *Heteranthera dubia*
- [ ] widgeon grass *Ruppia maritima*
- [ ] wild rice *Zizania aquatica*
- [ ] wild rye *Elymus virginicus*
- [ ] willows *Salix* spp.
- [ ] winterberry *Ilex verticillata*
- [ ] wood-nettle *Laportea canadensis*
- [ ] yellow iris *Iris pseudacorus*
- [ ] yellow pond lily *Nuphar advena*

About the Contributors

Juliana M. Barrett and Nels E. Barrett are well acquainted with the Connecticut River. Juliana and Nels both have done and are continuing to do ecological research that characterizes the rivers, landscape and vegetation. Juliana was formerly The Nature Conservancy's Geoffrey C. Hughes Tidelands Program Director. Nels is an ecologist with the Natural Resources Conservation Service. Juliana and Nels both hold doctorates in ecology.

Amy Cabaniss is Regional Recycling Coordinator for the Connecticut River Estuary Regional Planning Agency and started EHS Education, L.L.C in 1997. EHS provides environmental health and safety educational programs and products to communities across the country. As an environmental educator for 18 years and a Connecticut native, she enjoyed compiling the environmental organization resource list, and feels we are fortunate to have such a strong environmental community in the Connecticut River region.

David Allen Dunlop has been a faculty member at the Silvermine School of Art in Norwalk, Connecticut since 1993 and currently serves on its Board of Directors. A longtime river enthusiast and artist, David has painted and exhibited landscapes of river and marsh scenes in Connecticut for over 20 years. His work is nationally known and featured in many collections and fine art galleries throughout the country.

Stephen Gephard, though born and raised in Illinois, has spent most summers of his life canoeing and exploring the lower Connecticut River. Steve's family has owned a summer cottage on the river in Haddam for four generations. After graduating from college with a degree in biology, he moved to Connecticut and received a masters degree in fisheries biology from the University of Connecticut. His thesis investigated spawning runs of fish in the Salmon River in East Haddam. Steve has worked for the State of Connecticut Department of Environmental Protection-Fisheries Division since 1978. His primary responsibility is with the Atlantic Salmon Restoration Program and fishways. He currently supervises the Diadromous Fish Program for the Division and still can be commonly found weaving in and out of the coves and backwaters of the lower river, year-round.

Ellsworth S. Grant has sailed the Connecticut River and Long Island Sound for more than fifty years. He co-edited the first edition of the *Boating Guide to Long Island Sound.* Among his books are *The Miracle of Connecticut, Yankee Dreamers and Doers, The Colt Armory, and The City of Hartford.* His most recent book, *Thar She Goes!* is a history of shipbuilding on the Connecticut River.

Geoffrey A. Hammerson is a visiting associate professor of biology at Wesleyan University and a research zoologist with the Association for Biodiversity Information. Currently, Geoff is writing a book on the natural history of Connecticut.

Carol Hardin Kimball has been a summer resident of Hamburg for four decades. Since moving to Lyme full time in 1980 she has been moseying around the river's coves in her kayak. She is a docent at the Connecticut College Arboretum. Prior to this project, she served as the first planned giving officer at the Connecticut Chapter of The Nature Conservancy.

Thomas Maloney received a master's degree in resource management and administration from Antioch New England Graduate School in 1994, then took a job as Connecticut River Steward for the Connecticut River Watershed Council. In that position, he spearheaded a number of conservation initiatives, including restoration of migratory fishes to the tributaries of the Connecticut River. His knowledge and enthusiasm for the river, coupled with his love of kayaking the river's coves and marshes (and expertise in bird-watching), are evident in his writings. Tom now works with the Massachusetts Chapter of The Nature Conservancy, in Plymouth, Massachusetts.

Thomas Miner became Co-Executive Director of the Connecticut River Watershed Council in 1992 in partnership with his wife Whitty Sanford. Tom has directed conservation organizations in New York State and New England for the past 25 years. Under Tom and Whitty's leadership, the Watershed Council established the Connecticut River Steward Program and hired Tom Maloney as the first River Steward to provide a local, on-river presence for this watershed-wide organization.

John Pfeiffer is a lifelong resident of Old Lyme, Connecticut. John received his doctorate from the State University of New York at Albany. He has been a visiting lecturer at Wesleyan University since 1984. His research and dissertation concentrated upon the prehistoric archeology of the lower Connecticut River. In the past decade he has studied a shipwreck at the mouth of the Connecticut River, an early 17th-century Dutch fort at Branford, and historic shipyard and early industrial mill sites in Essex and Lyme. Today, he is the Old Lyme Town Historian and teaches aquaculture and habitat restoration in area high schools and universities. He is an avid birder and a member of the Old Lyme Conservation Trust, and is always delighted to get out on the river.

Noble Proctor is a professor of ornithology and botany at Southern Connecticut State University. Noble has explored the coves, marshes, and banks of the Connecticut River for nearly forty years, observing the birdlife and documenting the plant communities. A world traveler, he still feels that "the Connecticut River is one of the most beautiful rivers of the world." Noble is a resident of Branford and makes weekly visits to the river throughout the year.

Janet Radway Stone is a geologist with the U.S. Geological Survey (USGS) in East Hartford, Connecticut. She has worked for the USGS for more than 25 years, specializing in the glacial geology of New England. She is the author of numerous reports and maps about surficial geology, including the recent Quaternary Geologic Map of Connecticut and Long Island Sound Basin. She received her Bachelor of Arts degree from Birmingham Southern College and completed graduate studies at Wesleyan University.

Further Reading

Allen, Thomas B. *"Connecticut."* National Geographic, February 1994.

Bell, Michael. *The Face of Connecticut, People, Geology & the Land.* Hartford, CT: State of Connecticut, Department of Environmental Protection, Bulletin 110, Geological & Natural History Survey of Connecticut, 1985.

Bolling, David M. *How to Save a River: A Handbook for Citizen Action.* Washington, D.C.: River Network, Island Press, 1994.

Burt, Henry M. *Burt's Illustrated Guide of the Connecticut Valley.* Northampton, MA: New England Publishing, 1867.

The Complete Boating Guide to the Connecticut River. Easthampton, MA.: Connecticut River Watershed Council, Embassy Marine Publishing, 1990.

O 'Conniff, Richard. *"The Transformation of a River from 'Sewer' to Suburbs in 20 Years."* Smithsonian, April 1990.

Delaney, Edmund. *The Connecticut River: New England's Historic Waterway.* Essex, CT: The Connecticut River Foundation at Steamboat Dock, 1996.

Dreyer, Glenn D. and **William A. Neiring**. *Tidal Marshes of Long Island Sound, Ecology, History and Restoration.* New London, CT: Connecticut College Arboretum, Bulletin 34, 1995.

Dwight, Timothy. *Travels in New England and New York,* vol. II. Cambridge, MA: Harvard Univ. Press, 1969 (orig. 1821).

Ely, Susan H., and **Elizabeth B. Plimpton**. *The Lieutenant River.* Old Lyme, CT: Lyme Historical Society, 1991.

Glassberg, Jeffrey. *Butterflies through Binoculars.* New York: Oxford Univ. Press, 1993.

Grant, Ellsworth S. *"The Main Stream of New England."* American Heritage, April 1967.
　The Miracle of Connecticut. Hartford, CT: Connecticut Historical Society & Fenwick Publications, 1992.
　Thar She Goes! Essex, CT: Connecticut River Museum, 2000.

Harding, James Ely. *Lyme: As It Was and Is.* Lyme Bicentennial Commission,1976.
　Lyme Yesterdays: How Our Forefathers Made a Living on the Connecticut Shore. Stonington CT: The Pequot Press, 1967.

Hardy, David (et al). *50 Hikes in Connecticut.* Woodstock, VT: Backcountry Publications, 1996.

Hill, Evan, and **William F. Stekl**. *The Connecticut River.* Middletown, CT: Wesleyan Univ., 1972.

Hubbard, Ian. *Crossings: Three Centuries from Ferry Boats to the New Baldwin Bridge.* Lyme, CT: Greenwich Publishing Group, Inc., 1993.

Jorgensen, Neil. *A Sierra Club Naturalist's Guide: Southern New England.* San Francisco: Sierra Club, 1978.

Klemens, Michael W. *Amphibians and Reptiles of Connecticut and Adjacent Regions.* Hartford, CT: State of Connecticut, Department of Environmental Protection, Bulletin 112, Geological and Natural History Survey of Connecticut, 1993.

Little, Richard D. *Dinosaurs, Dunes, and Drifting Continents.* 2nd ed. Greenfield, MA: Valley Geology Pub., 1986.

Field Guide to the Birds of North America. Washington, D.C.: National Geographic Society, 1987.

Newcomb, Lawrence. *Wildflower Guide.* Boston: Little, Brown, and Company, 1977.

Peterson, Roger Tory. *A Field Guide to the Birds, Eastern and Central North America.* 4th ed. Boston: Houghton Mifflin, 1980.

Philips, David E. *Legendary Connecticut: Traditional Tales from the Nutmeg State.* Willimantic, CT: Curbstone Press, 1992.

Schuler, Stanley (ed.). *Hamburg Cove, Past and Present,* Old Lyme, CT: Lyme Historical Society, Florence Griswold Museum, 1993.

Sibley, David Allen. *The Sibley Guide to Birds.* National Audubon Society, Alfred A. Knopf, Inc., 2000.

Surowiecki, John. *A History of Connecticut's Coast.* Hartford: State of Connecticut, Department of Environmental Protection, Coastal Area Management Program, 1982.

Tiner, Ralph W. Jr., *Field Guide To Coastal Wetland Plants of the Northeastern United States.* Amherst: Univ. of Massachusetts Press, 1987.

Weiss, Howard M. *Marine Animals of Southern New England and New York.* Hartford, CT: State of Connecticut, Department of Environmental Protection, Bulletin 115, Geological & Natural History Survey of Connecticut, 1995.

Resource List

American Rivers, 1025 Vermont Avenue, NW, Suite 720, Washington, D.C. 20005, (202) 347-7550; Fax: (202) 347-9240; E-mail: amrivers@amrivers.org; www.amrivers.org

Mission: To protect and restore America's river systems and to foster a river stewardship ethic. Strives to secure a future in which healthy rivers support fish that are safe for human consumption and diverse species of wildlife and plant life; for recreation; and to improve the quality of life for all Americans.

Connecticut Audubon Society and Eco-tourism, Main Street, Essex, CT 06426, (860) 767-0660

Founded in 1898 by Mabel Osgood Wright as a small group of concerned citizens organized to protect birds, today this statewide Society that expands and enhances appreciation of all things that interact to form the great web of life. There are boundless opportunities to learn at Connecticut Audubon. Whether you hike nature trails, participate in a nature photography workshop, go eco-traveling, or volunteer as a teacher sharing your love of nature with young people, you'll quickly learn that Connecticut Audubon "isn't just for the birds…it's for you too"! Host of the annual, award-winning Eagle Festival in Essex, Connecticut.

Connecticut Fund for the Environment, 1032 Chapel Street, 3rd Floor, New Haven, CT 06510 (203) 787-0646, www.cfenv.org

CFE is a statewide environmental advocacy organization that uses science and the law to protect Connecticut's natural resources. CFE combines legal advocacy and public outreach to maximize its effectiveness. Since it's founding in 1978, CFE has saved wetlands, stopped unwise development, changed legislation, and won significant court battles.

Connecticut River Museum, 67 Main Street, Essex, CT 06426, (860) 767-8269; Fax: (860) 767-7028; E-mail: crm@connix.com; http://www.connix.com/~crm/

The mission of the Connecticut River Museum is to interest and educate all of the public in: the history, culture, and environment of the Connecticut River Valley and the use of the Connecticut River for commerce, natural habitat, and recreation.

Connecticut River Watch Program, Middlesex County Soil and Water Conservation District, Inc., 1066 Saybrook Road, P.O. Box 70, Haddam, CT 06438, (860) 345-3219; Fax: (860) 345-9175

Mission: To develop and support a network of community-based volunteer monitoring programs in the Connecticut River watershed in Connecticut, and to make water quality information more accessible to, and useable by, the general public and local officials.

Connecticut River Watershed Council, Inc., 15 Banks Road, Greenfield, MA 01301, (413) 772-2020; Fax: (413) 722-2090; E-mail: crwc@crocker.com; http://www.ctriver.org

The Connecticut River Watershed Council is the principal citizen advocate for the Connecticut River and its four-state watershed, New England's largest river ecosystem. Through education and stewardship, the Council works with businesses, nonprofits, institutions, schools, and government agencies to promote wise use, enjoyment, and habitat restoration.

Deep River Navigation Company & Mark Twain Cruises, P.O. Box 382, River Street, Deep River, CT. 06417, (860) 526-4954, or (877) MK TWAIN; www.deeprivernavigation.com

Runs daily Connecticut River cruises out of Deep River Landing, Old Saybrook, and Hartford, June through September. Lunch, buffet, and cocktail cruises available. Saturdays, January through March, enjoy an eagle-watching cruise out of Essex Steamboat Dock. Prices range from $8.00 to $28.00.

EHS Education, L.L.C., P.O. Box 647, Niantic, CT 06357-0647, (860) 691-0368; E-mail: ehse@uconect.net

EHS Education (EHSE) is dedicated to providing quality environmental, health, and safety education to communities nationwide. EHSE develops tailored educational products and programs on diverse topics such as solid waste management and coastal/marine ecology.

Land Trusts. For information on local land trusts in Chester, Deep River, east Haddam, Essex, Haddam, Lyme, Middlesex County, Old Lyme, and Old Saybrook, contact the Land Trust Service Bureau at the offices of the Nature Conservancy, 55 High Street, Middletown, CT 06457, (860) 344 0716, ext. 314.

Mattabeseck Audubon Society, 27 Washington Street, Middletown, CT 06457, (860) 685-2499; Fax: (860) 685-2241; E-mail: dtitus@wesleyan.edu

Mission: To provide environmental leadership and education for the benefit of the community and the Earth's biodiversity.

The Nature Conservancy, 55 High Street, Middletown, CT 06457, (860) 344-0716; www.tnc.org Tidelands and Coastal Marine office: 45 Main St., 2nd floor, Essex, CT. 06426, (860) 767-7706

Tidelands of the Connecticut River is a comprehensive program of The Nature Conservancy's Connecticut Chapter to protect the resources of the lower Connecticut River in Connecticut, specifically the tidal marshes, associated uplands, and the rare animals, plants, and natural communities that rely on them to survive. The Nature Conservancy has protected more than 4,000 acres in the Tidelands of the Connecticut River region. This program is part of the Conservancy's international "Last Great Places" initiative, which focuses on protecting large ecological systems in partnership with their human inhabitants.

Potapaug Audubon Society, P.O. Box 591, Old Lyme, CT 06371, (860) 767-1392; E-mail: enord@snet.net

Mission:To preserve and protect the environment and promote environmental awareness through education.

Rivers Alliance of Connecticut, Inc., 111 Main Street, Collinsville, CT 06022, (860) 693-1602; Fax:

(860) 693-6453; E-mail: rivers.alliance@snet.net; http://riversalliance.org

    RAC protects and restores rivers in Connecticut through support of regional water groups, public policy development, grassroots and volunteer action, and public education.

River Network, 153 State Street, Montpelier, VT, 05602, (802) 223-3840; www.rivernetwork.org

    River Network is a national organization whose mission is to "help people understand, protect and restore rivers and their watersheds." Founded in 1988 with the conviction that the solutions to river degradation are primarily local and must be created by citizen action watershed by watershed. Today, it continues to provide personalized assistance, training, and information to more than 500 partner groups through their watershed program.

The Valley Railroad, 1 Railroad Ave., Essex, CT, 06426, (860)767-0103; www.essexsteamtrain.com

    The Essex Steam Train runs daily steam-engine train and river boat rides (Deep River Navigation Company) from May through November, and most holidays. Special events include train and river boat rides for the annual Eagle Festival, Thomas the Tank Engine, and Theodore the Tugboat.

Government Departments and Agencies

Connecticut River Estuary Regional Planning Agency, 455 Boston Post Road, P. O. Box 778, Old Saybrook, CT 06475, (860) 388-3497; Fax: (860) 395-1404; E-mail: crerpa@snet.net

    CRERPA is dedicated to planning for, and promoting voluntary cooperative approaches to, changing land use and other issues affecting the character and people of the Connecticut River Estuary Region.

Connecticut River Gateway Commission, 455 Boston Post Road, P.O. Box 778, Old Saybrook, CT 06475, (860) 388-3497; Fax: (860) 395-1404; E-mail: crerpa@snet.net

    The Gateway Commission is an innovative combination of state, local, and private efforts striving to protect the Connecticut River valley. The Commission was authorized by the Connecticut General Assembly in 1973 and charged with the task of protecting the natural, aesthetic, and historic values of the lower Connecticut River Valley, which is one of the last unspoiled river estuaries on the Eastern Seaboard of the United States. Since its formation, the Commission has been instrumental in preserving scenic upland at key locations within the Conservation Zone.

Connecticut State Department of Environmental Protection, Marine Fisheries Headquarters, 33 Ferry Road, Old Lyme, CT. 06371, Main telephone (860) 434-6043, boating (860)434-8638

    The Marine Fisheries Headquarters is located in Ferry Landing State Park at the confluence of the Connecticut and Lieutenant rivers. Some of the docks are open for day use by boaters, and the piers are a popular spot for fishing and crabbing. Raised boardwalks along the marsh provide an enjoyable stroll, with interpretive signage detailing the natural history of the marsh.

Gillette Castle State Park, Lyme, CT, (860) 526-2336. Camping passes: (860) 424-3015.

    The park provides a public, car-top only boat launch on the Connecticut River (next to the Chester-Hadlyme Ferry), 122 acres of forest and trails, and the unique 1918 Gillette Castle, newly restored, that sits overlooking the Connecticut River on the hill known as "The Seventh Sister."

U.S. Fish and Wildlife Service, 300 Westgate Center Drive, Hadley, MA 01035-9589, (413) 253-8200; Fax: (413) 253-8456

    The U.S. Fish and Wildlife Service mission is to conserve, protect, and enhance fish and wildlife and their habitats for the continuing benefit of the American people. The Service's major responsibilities are for migratory birds, endangered species, certain marine mammals, and freshwater and anadromous fish.

U. S. Fish and Wildlife Service Silvio O. Conte National Fish and Wildlife Refuge, 38 Avenue A, Turners Falls, MA. 01376, (413) 863-0209; www.fws.gov/r5soc

    The goal of this unique refuge is to create the first national refuge that exists as a partnership between public and private lands, encompassing the whole of the Connecticut River watershed.

University of Connecticut Cooperative Extension System, 1066 Old Saybrook Road, P.O. Box 70, Haddam, CT 06438 (860) 345-4511; Fax: (860) 345-3357

    University of Connecticut CES Tidelands watershed projects are partnerships to protect and balance the unique natural resources and growth in the tidelands region. The projects are partnerships with the towns in the region, and state and federal agencies. The tidelands watershed projects are locally led, nonregulatory, and grounded in science and research.

This annotated resource list has been compiled by EHS Education, L.L.C.